Email Marketing Informer

Jon Crimes

Disclaimer

The author will not be responsible for any losses or damages of any kind incurred by the reader whether directly or indirectly arising from the use of the information found in this eBook. No guarantees of income are made or implied. The reader assumes responsibility for use of information contained herein.

ISBN-10: 1522714200
ISBN-13: 978-1522714200

Looking for a Special Bonus to really compliment this book?

Step 1: Visit www.JonCrimes.com

Step 2: Sign up to receive the free Email Series

Step 3: Get a PDF copy of this book and….

Step 4: Your great Free Bonus!

P.S. You're going to love it!

CONTENTS

MODULE 1 – INTRODUCTION

Welcome to the Email Marketing Informer.

My name is Jon Crimes and for past few years I've been making money through Affiliate Marketing and in particular, Amazon Affiliate Marketing.

At the beginning of 2014, I decided to branch out as a Marketer and started my own Blog: www.JonCrimes.com. As I developed this Internet Marketing (IM) Blog, I discovered a few things:

- I actually enjoy writing and helping others!
- IM can be a fun topic, honestly.
- Getting traffic to this Blog was going to be challenging (but by no means impossible).
- The visitors I did get were enjoying my work and leaving some great comments!

One of the biggest hurdles I faced however was how to create and manage an email list.

So why E-Mail Marketing?

In the past I've always been on the receiving end of email lists, some good with excellent information and some quite obviously just there to create money.

I even saw my email address being passed around other email marketers, even though the original marketer had ensured me that would never happen!

So here I was with a Blog which was looking good, giving value to my readers and building traffic quite nicely. But, I didn't have the first idea about how to engage visitors with an email list!

Does any of this sound familiar?

So the first big question I asked myself was, is learning about and implementing an email marketing strategy worth it?

You can find the answer to this very quickly on any of the IM Forums out there. My personal favourite (and that of countless others!) is the Warrior Forum (www.warriorforum.com).

Just to prove how topical email marketing still is and will be for a long time, look at Figure 1 which shows a screenshot of one particular thread in Warrior Forum:

	All-In-One: List Building Jassen		21st May 2014 09:34 AM by knowledge22	25	1,467	Main Internet Marketing Discussion Forum

FIGURE 1 - WARRIOR FORUM

This is a 'combined' thread on the Warrior Forum but it tells us that email marketing is a hugely popular topic and this particular thread has generated 1,467 views!

Email marketing is still recognised as one of the most important aspects of Internet Marketing and continues to develop a lot of interest amongst both experienced and newbie Internet Marketers.

But why is this?

As an Affiliate Marketer, promoting Amazon products, I was missing one big trick!

I knew how to write good review articles, how to get consistent traffic to my site and how to manage visitor/click conversions but there was one thing I didn't have any control over.

Once a visitor to my site had either clicked through to Amazon (made me a sale!) or just left my site completely without making that conversion, I lost them, possibly for ever!

The fact that they arrived at my site in the first place and that my Bounce Rate was low meant that I was doing many things right but I still wasn't making an attempt to capture that visitor and engage them on a more one to one basis.

In hindsight, I was missing a dedicated email marketing strategy.

How has Email Marketing worked for me?

Email marketing allows you to capture visitors arriving at your site, for me this has been the biggest change in the way I approach this business.

It's nice to know that all the hard work that goes into getting visitors to your site in the first place isn't wasted.

Even within just a few weeks of implementing a new Email marketing strategy on my site, I began to receive new subscribers to my all-important 'list'. Then I began the serious process of testing!

I found that including a good quality 'Lead Magnet' (more about these later!) started to attract not only more subscribers but also as I was offering a more niche specific freebee, my subscribers were becoming more targeted.

It became very apparent that the more targeted your list is, the less subscribers will opt-out from that list and providing you approach your email campaign right; you will keep the majority of these subscribers.

My list was building slowly but surely, with targeted subscribers who had subscribed to my emails by:

- Finding my blog whilst searching for related content
- Being interested in my niche specific Lead Magnet and making a decision that it was valuable enough to exchange for their email address
- Proving their interest in my content by following the 'double opt-in' email request

This has worked very well for me and there's no reason why it can't for you either.

How to follow these Modules?

What I've done with this guide is to write it in an order which reflects how I discovered the various pieces of the Email Marketing Jigsaw.

I would strongly advise you to read through the full guide first, without taking any notes or action. In fact, if possible read this guide from a portable device or print out a copy and ignore your main computer and the Internet for a while!

When learning new material, one of the biggest hurdles is terminology and this, in my opinion, is best mastered with no or very little distractions. No emails, no Facebook, nothing...

I've included a Glossary of Terms at the end of this book just to help beginners get to grips with the Internet Marketing language and for those (myself included) who need a little help with the memory!

This is a list of what remains in Email Marketing Informer:

Module 2 - Getting the Basics Right
All important, you need a good foundation before you even start thinking about Email Marketing. Maybe you already have a very strong Online Identity and a popular blog or website but for those that don't, or those that just want to see how I've done it, this Module will set you on the right track.

I'll also show you what platform I use for my blog and why I chose it, essential if you want to try and 'future proof' your online efforts.

And what about all that Legal Stuff? Are you concerned about CANSPAM, Affiliate Disclaimers or including your contact information? If not, please take a good look at this section, it might save you a lot of hassle and possibly a fortune!

Module 3 - Types of Email Campaigns
Now we go tactical!

What are the different types of email campaigns and which one is the most appropriate for your business?

Are you looking for a purely 'Authority' based marketing campaign, 'Pure Money Making' or a combination of the two?

Maybe you know what I'm talking about, maybe you don't! After this module you'll know which one is right for you.

Module 4 - Breakdown of an Effective Email Message
This is where you start to understand what makes up an effective email.

We look at the Header, the Body, having that all important 'call to action', the importance of having an unsubscribe option and including your contact details in the email. Why is all that important? Let me tell you.

Module 5 - Getting Subscribers
Time to get your hands dirty.

Let me show you how to 'know your audience', create excitement and make that all important 'capture'.

What do you know about Lead Magnets? After Module 5 you'll know all you need to know.

We'll also talk about opt-in's, opt-outs and Autoresponders.

Module 6 - Increasing Traffic
Free or Paid? Firstly you need to know what the options are and then you can make a decision on what's right for you.

I'll show you what's worked for me and also what hasn't! Let me help you find the right traffic sources for your Email marketing campaign.

Module 7 - Keeping Subscribers
Don't throw all that hard work away!

The importance of a good 'Thank you' page. Get your Subscriber to

'Whitelist' you and find out exactly who's opening their emails!

Analytics! Where are your subscribers coming from? Reviewing the Geography and Demographics of your main subscriber base can be very useful in optimising your email campaign; this module takes the mystery out of this very useful tool.

Module 8 - Advanced Techniques

In Advanced Techniques I'll show you the benefit of using Swipe Files, explain what A/B Split Testing is and what to test.

We'll look at how you can manage subscribers on more than one list with Automated Rules and how an email marketing service can make this really easy!

You'll also see how to create a Segment with your list and we'll discuss some of the best ways to combine a Broadcast with your Autoresponder emails.

MODULE 2 – GETTING THE BASICS RIGHT

Your Online Identity

Whether you're email marketing, selling physical or digital products online or providing a service to others, it's vital that you have some form of identity online.

This can be as simple as just having a single social media account, a Facebook account for instance, or going full blown with your own blog site, your name in your URL, multiple social media accounts (in your name!) and taking every available opportunity to build your online identity.

Let me give you a couple of scenarios?

Scenario 1
Whilst reading a well-known Internet Marketing Forum you've come across an Internet Marketer called Bob Deacon. You like what he has to say, he appears to know his stuff and you are wondering whether to click on his Forum Signature which promises a brand new 'How to make money online' series of emails from Bob Deacon.

But before you do, you decide to try and find out a bit more about Bob Deacon online, so you do a search for him on Google.

Nothing....Apart from, his name appears against a search entry for that forum. Not convinced, you decide that you might join his email list later but decide to do some more reading on some other forums first, Bob Deacon is quickly forgotten about.

Scenario 2
In this scenario, you've come across an Internet Marketer called Alex Knight.

You found him on the same IM Forum and he's offering something similar to Bob but this time you get some very interesting results when you do a search for his name!

You find that he is quite active online with a Blog and Social Media Accounts, some of which are on page 1 of Google.

You can even visit his blog, check out the quality of his work, subscribe to his email list to find out a bit more about him and what he offers to visitors to his site and make a decision on whether you believe his claims on the IM Forum where you first spotted him!

Sorry for the obvious question but you have a choice between these two Internet Marketers.

Who would you rather invest your time and/or money in?

Quick summary
Online identity is very important. Even if you're just starting out with an online business, be it Internet Marketing or selling physical products, it's relatively easy to get an online identity, and fast!

Tips for Developing your Online Identity

1. Be yourself
No matter what your name is, do you really want to use a pen name if you want to have an honest and trustworthy online presence?
My advice here is to use your own name or company identity from the outset wherever possible.

2. Buy a URL which includes your name or business identity
When I first started my Internet Marketing Blog, I was unsure whether I should actually use my surname for the URL and Blog.

My surname, Crimes, initially looked like a difficult name to rank in Google with all the bad news that such a name brings to the search results!

Luckily I was persuaded to give it a try and was further reassured that once you start adding good, relevant content to your blog, on a consistent basis, you soon start to get some traction over even the most high profile search results!

This advice proved excellent.

It took a few weeks but I found my Blog at the top of Page 1, very reassuring for anyone doing a search on my name.

So, buy a URL, preferably with your name in it. For example: www.joncrimes.com/blog

3. Start your own Internet Marketing Blog
This has to be one of the best ways to show off what you can do and what you know!

Of course, creating a Blog is a huge topic in itself and not within the scope of this eBook but let me point you in the right direction.

I used the Bloggers Roadmap to help me setup and develop my Blog and if you haven't done so already, check out my Blog:

http://www.joncrimes.com/blog/

and see exactly what this Roadmap has done for me.

I think the Bloggers Roadmap (www.bloggersroadmap.com) is without a doubt one of the best Blog creation guides available today.

It saved me so much time and money in the initial stages and helped me get a Blog up and running which was capable of capturing visitors to my blog and turning them into subscribers by using a good Lead Magnet, in this case a Free Report (more about Lead Magnets later!).

If you haven't checked out the Free Bloggers Roadmap report yet then you can do so here:
www.bloggersroadmap.com

4. Branding - Header & Graphics

So you've setup your blog, the address for which happens to include your name, all good.

Now, when a visitor arrives at your site, excellent content alone isn't going to reinforce your name and ultimately your 'brand'.

For this you need to create that good first impression and that's where a Header comes in.
You can find loads of examples out there of how a decent Header reinforces brand and can actually make or break a site.

Again, I think the best way to give you a suitable example is to demonstrate by experience. Back to my Blog!

Initially, I tried to make my own Header. I've done it with affiliate sites before but they have been 'acceptable' at best. My attempts to make a suitable branding Header for my new 'hub' just weren't good enough.

Advice: Unless you're very good at designing Graphics for websites, this includes Headers, and can do so quickly, then please doesn't waste your time and effort on trying to get this right!

Just find the right person or company to do it for you and outsource. I found a company called GFX-1 to create a Header for me and they come highly recommended.

With my Blog, I wanted the Header to build on the common interpretation of my surname and have a 'Crime Scene' feel to it! Of course, it still needed to have an Internet Marketing theme as well otherwise visitors would get seriously confused when they arrived at my site!

These were the very 'vague' instructions' which I gave to GFX-1, all this late on a Friday afternoon. Less than 24 hours later they had some suggestions for me to look at and I had the Header installed on my site that very same day.

Do you think my Blog Header builds a brand around my name whilst giving the visitor confidence that they've arrived at an Internet Marketing site?

FIGURE 2 - HEADER GRAPHICS

You can check out the services GFX-1 offer through this link:

www.EmailMarketingInformer.com/Recommends-GFX-1

5. Content
You've probably seen it yourself. Good looking Blogs which at one time received regular, consistent and relevant content, then it all stopped!
There are many reasons for this of course but you can't afford to follow this trend!

Your Blog needs this content as long as you need the Blog...
Initially, you don't need to concentrate too much on keyword research, writing style or anything to fussy, you just need to produce content that your visitors find useful and interesting.

More than anything, this initial content is doing 2 things:

1. It's getting you in the habit (or back in the habit!) of writing
2. You're adding your personality to your brand

So for example, you're initial posts can be:

- An introduction - who are you?
- You're experiences in Internet Marketing (or your chosen niche)
- What this site is all about?
- How it's going to benefit your readers?

You can write a post that gives a good summary of your niche.

Break it down into sub-headings and introduce the different aspects of your chosen field.

Then write some posts on some of the niche topics that you have direct experience with.

But whatever you write about, just make sure you add good content on a regular basis. To me this was (and still is!) one good post a week. You can do more than that of course but it's important to make sure that this content is of very good quality.

Just remember that you need to give considerable value to your visitors and that Google would very much like to see an active site with content being added on a fairly frequent basis!

But always put your visitors first!

The Right Platform

If you've managed to have a look at the Bloggers Roadmap, you'll notice that the guidelines for developing a blog are all centred around WordPress.

This is one of the most popular Content Management Systems (CMS) today and you'll find many examples online of successful blogs and websites that use WordPress.
My advice to you is to follow success! Do what the best do and use WordPress.

If you've never used WordPress before then please don't panic, it doesn't take long to master the basics and even the more advanced stuff can be learnt relatively quickly.

You can read more about WordPress through this link which takes you straight to their 'Support Everything' User Manual:

https://make.wordpress.org/support/user-manual/

Legal Stuff

CAN-SPAM

This is a US Government act that was signed in 2003 and as the name suggests, is very much anti-spam.

It actually stands for: *Controlling the Assault of Non-Solicited Pornography and Marketing* but is essentially a set of standards aimed at emails with a commercial intent and even if you have no connection with the USA, these standards are very much worth following.

For a more detailed look at CAN-SPAM, take a look here:

www.fcc.gov/guides/spam-unwanted-text-messages-and-email

but to give you a flavour of what this act entails, commercial emails must adhere to the following.

- They must make available and honour unsubscribe requests. This option should be below the main email body text and should be clearly visible.
- Content of emails should be accurate.
- Emails should have a legitimate physical address displayed.
- Good email sending behaviour should be adopted, for example: No false headers

There is of course more to CAN-SPAM than this brief summary but I hope you get the idea.

A lot of this is common sense of course but there are also ways in which compliance can be made a lot easier!

Email Autoresponder Providers, such as Aweber, automatically manage the unsubscribe function for you, include your physical address in your email and also give you a SPAM score (just in case you forget to be good!).

My advice, choose a decent Email Provider (more of this later).

Make sure you understand the CAN-SPAM rules and play fair!

Affiliate Disclaimers

These days it's common place for a blogger, website owner or email marketer to promote affiliate offers in their content.

The trick of course is not to overload your readers and visitors too much with all of these 'fantastic' offers but there's also another aspect of affiliate marketing which is equally important.

....

Disclaimers

....

People know that at some point they're going to be confronted with a recommendation or special offer that is going to earn the recommender a commission.

But, it's great when that person makes it clear on their site or in their email that this might well happen. It basically demonstrates honesty and maybe more importantly, you actually care about the person who is reading your material.

If you get in the habit of using Disclaimers from day one then it'll become very natural to everything you do online.

It gets even easier!

If you use one of the main Email Autoresponder Services, then you can create an email template that includes this Disclaimer in it. So when you come to add a new email to your autoresponder series or 'broadcast' a special to your list, the Disclaimer is already there!

So what's a good Disclaimer to add to your email?
Again, please be patient!

I'm going to include a Disclaimer example when we look at Module 4 (Breakdown of an effective email message).

So what about adding Disclaimers to your blog or site?

Well, here you have a number of options.
You can have a look at other peoples sites (mine for instance!) and use their Disclaimers as a basis for yours, or:

If your using WordPress then you can pay a little bit of money and buy this fantastic legal plugin called InstaLegalPages.

This can save you a ton of time and it is something which I installed on my blog from day 1, why waste time trying to write all the legal stuff yourself?

You can check it out here:

http://instalegalpages.com/

Most Important Disclaimer

I'm going to state the obvious here but please bear in mind that nothing of what I've said here constitutes legal advice.

This is my opinion only but everything I've mentioned about Disclaimers here has been tried and tested without any problems.

If in doubt though, please seek professional legal advice.

Contact Information

We touched on this in CAN-SPAM where you're required (strongly advised!) to include a correct physical address in any emails which have a commercial intent.

We also mentioned that Email Autoresponder Providers such as Aweber will even do this automatically for you.

In my opinion though, including your physical address in emails has an even more important purpose, it generates trust!

This links back to developing your online identity and being a real person, with a real address.

Word of advice here, not everyone has their physical address attached to everything they do online but if you do decide to include it on your blog/site as well as your emails, please make sure they match!

I've seen countless examples where this is not the case and it's amazing how all that hard work to build trust and identity can be destroyed so very quickly in the eyes of your readers and visitors.

MODULE 3 – TYPES OF EMAIL CAMPAIGNS

In this module we'll be looking at the different types of email campaigns that you can use for your business.

When I say different types, I've only seen 3 different types of campaign but the 3rd one can take a number of forms, let me explain.

The 3 different types of email campaign are:

- Authority Building Campaign
- Pure Money Making Campaign
- The Hybrid!

Authority Building Campaign

Building up Authority goes a long way to making a success with your online activities and a good way to build on this authority quickly is with your email campaign.

If you're in the position where you're just starting out as an Internet Marketer and you've built your blog and collected you're first group of subscribers, then the last thing you want to be doing is bombarding them with offers and 'buy now' specials when you haven't built up that all important authority and trust!

This is where the Authority Building Email Campaign comes in.

In the short term, you want to be treating your subscribers to real value!

Maybe your subscribers were taken in by your excellent blog content or maybe it was the fantastic free gift you were offering them in exchange for their email (more about Lead Magnets later), either way they are curious about what your email list can do for them and you don't want to disappoint.

Give them exactly what they want, good quality information that solves a problem they might have.

Pure Money Making Campaign

I tried to do this and it didn't work for me but that's not to say it hasn't been successful for other Internet Marketers.

With this type of campaign, you are purely interested in making money from your subscribers and all of your emails will be written with this in mind.

That's not to say that these type of campaigns don't have good information in them, some do, but any information, hints, tips or 'recommendations' will target your subscriber to click a well-placed link and make you a commission.

I've seen many types of campaigns which fall into this category, as you might have, and some are very clever in the way they draw the reader in and entice them to '*find out more here*!'

However, I have never been able to fully trust the Marketers behind these emails unless I know them personally, they have been recommended to me or through good quality products they have created in the past.

I'm very much in the frame of mind that you need to build an element of trust before trying to empty your subscriber's wallet; maybe this could be called a 'Hybrid' method?

Hybrid Campaign

There's absolutely nothing wrong with having the best of both worlds and this is what I found really started to work for me.

Initially a subscriber to my list would be 'treated' to emails which gave them considerable value. These would include:

- Advice on how to do a particular task within that niche.

- Introducing a problem that they might or might not come across yet and then solving that problem for them in a subsequent email.

- Asking them if there is anything they would like advice on or would like to see included in future emails (make them feel part of the process!)

- Recommending tools for that niche. These could be free or paid tools but I would make a point of explaining to my reader that I am only recommending this because I have used it and it works and that the link they click on is for more information and not an affiliate link (great for building up trust!)

- Niche news or samples of your latest posts/articles.

So that would essentially be the 'Authority' part of the Hybrid Campaign at work!

For me, I would never go straight into Pure Money Making even after building up considerable trust with my readers.

However, if you're in this to make money then you obviously need to introduce this part into your Hybrid Campaign at some point.

A great way to do this is to start introducing your readers to services and tools that you have personally used and can fully recommend but this time use affiliate links for the click through.

We didn't do it in the 'Authority Building' stage because the main purpose of this was to build trust but now that you've got that trust, most people appreciate that giving the author of the email a small commission in return for their efforts is perfectly acceptable.

Do you tell the reader that this an affiliate link?

Personally I don't tell them directly next to the link but I have seen others do so. I don't think it's that important at this stage and could possibly distract your reader from clicking on the link in the first place.

What is important though is to:

- Make sure that your recommendation is genuine. Never recommend a product that you haven't tried yourself, if it turns out to be a poor product, service or tool then your reputation could really suffer.
- Make sure that you have an affiliate disclaimer in your email, usually placed at the bottom of the email.

Along with the introduction of affiliate links in recommendation emails, you should also continue to give them emails that have useful information that's going to get them excited when they see your next message arrive in their inbox.

As you continue to build trust with your subscribers, you can introduce more and more product recommendations and slowly move the ratio in favour of Pure Money Making as opposed to Authority Building. It's still important though to include emails that offer value to your readers without turning all your messages into sales letters.

MODULE 4 – BREAKDOWN OF AN EFFECTIVE EMAIL MESSAGE

In this Module we're going to breakdown an effective email into its various parts.

These include:

1. The Headline
2. Body
3. Take Action
4. Unsubscribe
5. Contact Details
6. Social Triggers
7. Disclaimer

Now before we start, some of these message 'functions' have flexible positions in an email message and the 'Take Action' function for example can float anywhere in the email and is quite often repeated!

Some other functions are also flexible and it is not uncommon to see Social Triggers (Facebook/Twitter Share Buttons etc.) just below a signature in some emails or write at the bottom of an email in others!

What I'm trying to say here is that not everything is set solid.

So let's breakdown that email.

The Headline

The Headline has one primary purpose, to get your email opened!

It really doesn't matter how good your content is if no one actually gets to see it so the Headline needs to be right!

It needs to be short enough to be instantly readably yet have enough information to give your reader exactly what they need to know, 'what am I going to get when I open this message!'

Make it personal!

I find that if your message has that personal touch then it's more likely to get opened. For example, my subscribers name is Mark, my headline might read something like:

"Mark, great news! Social Media just got EASY..."

Personalising your messages is itself quite easy these days, especially with Autoresponder services like Aweber.

Let's have a look at some engaging Headlines which have been proven to work:

"Steve, don't miss out – Final hours to save big!"

"Hi Judy, time is running out, FB Ads made easy…"

"Naomi, here's 3 ways to improve your Social Media…"

"Clinton, 5 jaw-dropping traffic tips, check this out…"

"Email subscriber exclusive: Traffic Heaven, 75% off NOW…"

I'll be honest, I made up the names but the general format of these emails has worked for me and it's all about grabbing their attention and trying to stand out from the crowd!

A strict rule that I've tried to stick to is not to give false promises, especially in your headline.

How many times have you seen an email with a message headline that promises riches beyond belief, all for just 20 minutes a day (or similar)?

If it sounds too good to be true, most people will hit the delete key.

Engage honestly!

The Body

So your headline has done its job and the email has been opened but now you need to catch your subscriber's attention again and keep them interested.

It's important to build on your headline quickly in the body of your message.

For example, here's a message which I have used for one of my lists (I've used 'Mark' as an example again!):

Headline:
"Mark, do you Guest Post? Get Massive Traffic and Authority quickly!"

Body:
"Limited budget but need fast targeted traffic?
I've got your back!
Believe me, you already have the skills to do this, you just need to concentrate your energy on something that really works, Guest Posting.
...."

The Body naturally follows on from the Headline and this is what you need to do with your messages. Personally, I've read email message bodies which don't relate to the Headline in any way or form and that is a big no-no.

There is no point in just trying to be clever with your Headline, catch the attention and build a bit of trust with your subscriber, only to let them down when they start reading the email body.

We're not in the business of trying to fool people, what we really want to do is build up trust and authority with our readers.

Take Action

Your 'Take Action' obviously needs to be clear to your reader but not at the expense of the information which introduces that action.

For example, this next message has the 'Take Action' displayed in the second paragraph, whilst the first paragraph builds up the interest level for the reader:

"Mark, Flip your site for PROFIT!"

"Are you interested in finding out how much money you can make by flipping your site?

With this FAIL PROOF method you can make huge money by flipping your site and get that big payday that your hard work thoroughly deserves. It really is a no brainer!

CLICK HERE TO DOWNLOAD 'FLIP MANIAC' TODAY

In this video series I'll show you how to...."

So again, the Body has followed on from the Headline and the first paragraph begins to build up the product, getting the reader ready for that all important 'Take Action', which in this case is the 'CLICK HERE...' sentence.

After this first 'Take Action', the email then starts to give a summary of exactly what this product does.

It's important to include a second 'Take Action' at the end of the message as well (or very near the end!). A lot of readers, even if interested, will want to read more about this fantastic product and what it can do for them but will need to be reminded about what they need to do to get themselves a copy!

So the end of your email message could look something like:

"...by following this series of videos and taking action today, 'Flip Maniac' can show you how to flip websites and make a hefty profit along the way!
CLICK HERE TO DOWNLOAD 'FLIP MANIAC' TODAY"

By the way, I haven't got exclusive rights to a product called Flip Maniac and as far as I can tell, no one has. Please feel free to use it!

Your 'Take Action' needs to have a sense of urgency about it without appearing too pushy!

You can see that I've used 'Today' in the example above. This is a good example of this urgency but you could also use many other words, such as:

- Now
- While stocks last
- With HUGE Discount until ...
- Don't miss this one time offer!

You probably get the picture?

The 'Take Action' is as equally as important as the Headline and the message Body. You need to get all these pieces right to keep your email open rates and conversions as high as possible.

Unsubscribe

Giving your subscriber the option to say 'goodbye' is mentioned a few times in Email Marketing Informer!

Two main reasons:

1. Making sure you have this option in your emails means you are complying with one of the CAN-SPAM guidelines.
2. Professionalism. You shouldn't be running an email campaign with the primary goal of trying to spam people.

If they find they are not interested in remaining as one of your subscribers then they should have a clear way of unsubscribing from your list.

Better a lost subscriber than someone who is going to complain to your email service provider that you have been spamming them!

So where do you put the 'Unsubscribe' link?

If you use one of the big email service providers, then this option is already taken care for you and you'll find an 'Unsubscribe' link at the bottom of your emails.

If you don't use such a service then I would still advise you to place this link at the very end of your emails. It seems to be where people look for such an option these days anyway and it won't interrupt the natural flow of your message.

It is there purely as an option for anyone who doesn't want to be on your list anymore!

Contact Details

Similar in reasons to the 'Unsubscribe' link, displaying your (real) contact details in your email is another one of the CAN-SPAM guidelines and it also adds that extra professional touch to your emails.

And again, services like Aweber will do this automatically for you by using your account details for that service.

These details need to be added to the bottom of your email as well.

Social Triggers

Social Media like Facebook, Twitter, Pintrest and LinkedIn are slowly starting to move into the email world and for a very good reason!

Start writing emails that offer great value to your readers, with or without offers attached, and you might find that one of your subscribers wants to share this with their friends!

However, for many of us, forwarding that email might seem like a task to far and before you know it, that moment of interest is lost.

Enter your Social Triggers

Now your reader only has to click on the 'Share' button in your email for whatever Social Media takes their fancy and your message is starting to go viral!

Whether people are getting more busy, lazy, or both, we need to cater for this in our emails.

Where to place Social Triggers?

An obvious place is just below your 'signature' after the main body of the email but you can also include these triggers in the content as well.

Social Trigger options vary between email autoresponder service providers so you'll have to see what options your service has.

A good example of this is with the Aweber Drag & Drop Email Builder which allows you to add "Follow Me" buttons into your email message that link direct to your Facebook or Twitter pages.

Other major providers will have a similar option.

Disclaimer

I used to think (many years ago!) that including disclaimers in content would be a huge turnoff for my readers.

I now think completely the opposite. Adding disclaimers to your email messages also adds a degree of trust in your communication. You're basically being upfront in your activities and not trying to hide anything.

Have you ever received an email which is quite obviously been written with the sole intent of making the author money? I have and with no disclaimers visible either! Face it, that person is not interested in developing a trust relationship with you; they just want to get hold of your cash.

Now, you receive an email that has good quality information in it. It also has a 'Take Action' link which has a sense of urgency about it without being overly pushy and this link is directly related to the content.

You've built up a level of trust with your subscriber and they probably already appreciate that some of your links are going to be for Affiliate payments.

Now, when they get to the end of the message, they see an Affiliate Disclaimer statement. The level of trust increases and your reader knows exactly what that link will do for them (the message content will tell them that) and what that link will do for you.

Good exchange.

MODULE 5 – GETTING SUBSCRIBERS

Know your audience

Who do you want to subscribe?

That's a good question! When I first started building a list, my answer to this was 'everyone' but this couldn't be further from the truth.

For an email list to be effective, it needs to be targeted towards the right people and for a number of reasons:

1. For many email autoresponder services, you pay more for that service as your list grows past certain limits. You certainly don't want to be paying for uninterested subscribers!

2. You also don't want subscribers to start complaining that you are spamming them! Obviously you won't be sending out spam on purpose but if you have subscribers who are not really interested in your material then they might interpret it as spam anyway. This is a very important point as the more complaints you get, the more it can affect the delivery of your future emails!

3. A smaller list with genuinely interested people who look forward to your emails is always going to convert better that a huge list full of random 'subscribers' who only really signed up for the initial freebie and couldn't even be bothered to unsubscribe afterwards! If unsubscribing is too much effort for them, are they really going to show interest in your emails and make a future purchase?

What do they want?

This question has many factors and sometimes the only way you're really going to know what your subscribers want is to ask them.

You've already got a head start of course providing that you've been able to attract the right people to your site in the first place and you've encouraged them to subscribe to your mailing list with an appropriate Lead Magnet (more about Lead Magnets later).

If we use the example of an Internet Marketing Blog, then of course the majority of people who arrive at the site are going to be interested in Internet Marketing related information.

When I think of what my subscribers want, I normally follow 3 important steps:

1. Make sure my site is clear in what it's about! If it's a website about Dog Training, then that will be reflected in the sites URL, the site header and the opening text on the front page. I don't what to give visitors any chance in being confused about where they are. If they want to know about Dog Training then they've come to the right place and there'll be mutual benefit from making them email subscribers. Otherwise, why we should waste each other's time?

2. Make your subscribers Lead Magnet appropriate to the material you will be sending them when they subscribe. For example, with the Dog Training site again, if you have a subscription form which promises owners of 'Small Dogs' a free guide which will solve all their training problems for Angelo the little Bichon Frise, then are they really going to be interested in an email series about how to groom the world's largest dogs? Bottom line, if a visitor becomes a subscriber to your email list by being 'enticed' by your offer, then we should be getting a good idea about what they want.

Always have a link in your email where subscribers can get in touch with you directly! It's a good idea to have this towards the end of the email message, in the 'admin' area of the email and to introduce the link something like:

"Want to know something which hasn't been included in this email? For questions, comments or feedback please get in touch direct at

Jon@emailmarketinginformer.com"

This of course works well for both parties. Your subscriber feels more valued and less inclined to think they're receiving emails from a robot and you get some great ideas for new email content!

Create Excitement

If you find that you're getting traffic to your site but not much in the way of subscribers then it's time to review how you're trying to 'catch' your subscribers!

Let's assume that the traffic you're getting is targeted and that your subscription form has an appropriate and desirable Lead Magnet but you feel that you could be doing better in terms of subscriber numbers!

Maybe you need to create some excitement on your site and get your visitors all hot and bothered about signing up to your email list.

Creating a Quiz

Most people like a good quiz and they like it even more when they're given a chance to show how 'knowledgeable' they are in a particular subject!

With most quiz applications you can set them up so that the person doing the quiz has to give their email address to see the results of the quiz.

You could even promise a 'top prize' for the first person to get 'full marks' on the quiz.

Introducing a quiz onto your site to get more interest from visitors and ultimately get extra subscribers is a great way to build your email list and quickly. Like everything else though, it needs some testing to get right and it might take some different versions of the quiz before it becomes really effective.

If you're using WordPress, I recommend trying out a plugin called 'SlickQuiz', easy to use and produces some nice quizzes.

You can check it out here:

https://wordpress.org/plugins/slickquiz/

How about holding a competition on your website?

Another way to generate interest on your site and capture email addresses is to hold a competition.

This can be pretty much anything and the prize (or prizes!) can range from something as simple as a free eBook to the latest gadget or even something much bigger!

What's important here though is that the competition, prize and expectation are appropriate to the kind of email subscribers that you want for your list.

How about an example?

You have a website about motorbikes and hold a competition where you ask people to write, in 500 words, where they would like to ride a Harley Davidson. The prize by the way is a Harley Davidson 'weekend experience'.

You get loads of interest through this competition and collect many emails. Then you start your email campaign and it is full of useful information about 'Speed Bikes' and how to generally go faster in everything you do!

Is this going to appeal to someone who has taken the time to write 500 words about 'Easy Riding across Route 66'? Maybe, maybe not but it's definitely not as targeted as it could be and with this sort of mixed strategy you would expect to see quite a few unsubscribers.

Keep it all relevant.

Email Capture

Email Subscription Form

There's a few different ways to collect subscribers email addresses but probably the most common is by using an Email Subscription Form.

If you're using an email marketing service like Aweber or

then getting an email subscription form on your site and properly setup is made a lot easier.
Also, the bigger services like Aweber have a good selection of subscription form templates which are editable and can be made to fit in with the color and theme of your site with relative ease.

If you're thinking of using an email subscription form then it's also a great idea to have a look at some of the popular websites in your niche to see how they have included this form within their site.

Some questions to ask yourself:

1. How are they enticing visitors to part with their email address?

2. How prominent is this subscription form in relation to other content on that page?

3. Is this form on every page of their site?

It might also be a good idea to subscribe to a few of the more popular websites in your niche and follow their process and emails. It can give you some great ideas!

The Pop-up!

The Pop-up can be used as an extra way to get visitors to subscribe to your email list.

Pop-ups seem to have a love or hate relationship, especially with Internet Marketers. Used correctly however, they can very effective and the beauty with these is that you can test them a lot easier than the traditional subscription form and change when (or where) they appear.

For example, on my Internet Marketing Blog, I had a Pop-up which was set to display when a new visitor arrived at my site and then only every 7 days if that visitor returned. So, if that visitor happened to find the information on my site interesting, and they returned daily, then they wouldn't be bombarded with the Pop Up every time they visited the site.

To me, this was very important as I didn't want to push the visitor away because they felt like they were being 'over-sold' too!

Pop-ups can be effectively managed through the big email marketing services and my advice would always be to start with these at the beginning.

Squeeze Page

Now a Squeeze Page is a page that is designed to obtain someone's name and email address, usually in exchange for a free report or something else which the visitor to that page might find valuable.

Sounds similar to the email subscription form right?

Many websites find that by combining these two methods, the opt-in rate for that site is much better than if a traditional email subscription form is used alone!

If you haven't tried to create a Squeeze Page for your site yet then I would strongly advise that you at least give it a go and test to see how much difference it makes to getting email subscribers.

The Lead Magnet

This is probably the single most important part of your quest to gain subscribers to your list.

The Lead Magnet is very simply an offer (or enticement) to make visitors to your website leave their email address and join your email list in return for some information which is of value to them.

The Lead Magnet is an essential part of having a successful email list and it's important to get it right from the beginning by asking yourself a few questions:

1. What's going to be of value to visitors on my site? Put yourself in their position and when you arrive at the site and something really stands out as a 'must have', are you going to be more inclined to exchange that gift for your email address? Probably!

2. Is what you're offering going to be compatible with your email list? It doesn't have to be an exact match of course but you really need to be in the same ballpark at least! What you're aiming for here is a subscriber who really wanted your Lead Magnet so bad that they were willing to take a chance on you and 'surrender' their email address. You also want them to have a genuine interest in the content that you will be giving them as part of their daily/weekly emails. Just make sure the two things aren't too different!

3. Is your Lead Magnet going to attract just a bunch of 'free gift' seekers? This is where you need to be careful because you don't want a bunch of unsubscribers or even worse, complaints to your email service provider about SPAM. You need to take a bit of time to think carefully about the Lead you're offering and this goes back to the previous question where we talked about making sure the Lead Magnet and your email content is compatible! Try and make the Lead Magnet targeted and appropriate for the audience.

What sort of Lead Magnet should you use?

Before we go into that, there's one more thing which you need to keep at the front of your find as far as Lead Magnets go:

They need to stand out from the crowd!

Think about it, you're asking visitors to part with that most precious of internet identities, their email address. For some sites, the brand name, reputation or just the quality and quantity of the content might be enough to get those subscribers. For the rest of us mere mortals, we have to offer the visitor something really attractive in return for their contact details.

Here are some ideas about things you can use as Lead Magnets:

- A 'free' report. Possibly the most popular Lead Magnet?
- An eBook
- A Plugin or some other form of software, exclusive to your site!
- An audio interview. Maybe an interview from a 'big name' in your chosen subject.
- A video (how-to series)
- A mentoring package. Would your visitors benefit from being able to ask you questions direct?
- Coupons or Offers. Great for retail sites and maybe other niches as well. Is there a product which your visitors might find attractive and you can get an exclusive discount for them?
- Online Webinar. Put your knowledge to good use and create a series of Webinars! Offer these as a 'Gift' to your loyal subscribers.
- Similar with the Webinar but instead create a series of Podcasts and include the first one as a signup 'bonus' to your visitor. Links to future Podcasts can be included in your email series.
- Test them! People love a quiz. How about getting them to test themselves and find out exactly how much they know? In return for their contact details of course!

Outsource or DIY Lead Magnets?

Good question. Ideally you would want to do it yourself but if you do decide to outsource this task then I would strongly advise that you at least review and inject some of your personality into the 'product' after it has been completed.

Outsourcing is of course a great way to save that most valuable of things, time, and I would be the first person to advise employing someone else to help with your business wherever you can, money permitting of course.

If you don't already have the ideas and at least some of the material in place already to create your Lead Magnet then it's worth considering using the services of another writer who can create this product for you and then you can add your own 'personal touches' afterwards.

Some great resources for doing this include:

Warrior Forum
iWriter
Elance

I've personally had the most success with Fiverr and iWriter for creating content, it can sometimes be a matter of trial and error though!

Email Opt-in

Always use an Email double opt-in. Let me explain why?

Gone are the days when you just wanted as many people on your list as possible and you didn't really care about unsubscribers or people reporting your emails as SPAM!

This is the quick way to get noticed for the wrong reasons and before you know it; your email marketing service will start to see you as 'undesirable'. In turn, that could have an adverse effect on your email delivery rates.

What you need to do is do your best to make sure that anyone who joins your list has a genuine interest in being on it and that when you start your actual email campaign and send them emails; they are more unlikely to unsubscribe or report you as SPAM!

The Double Opt-in

With the major email marketing services, like Aweber, Mail Chimp or Get Response, you have the option to set this up automatically when you start building your email campaign.

Then when a visitor likes the look of your Lead Magnet (or Pop-Up/Squeeze Page etc.), and 'applies' to join your list by handing over their email address, a second Opt-In is initiated by your email marketing service.

Your subscriber receives an email which informs them that they must click on a link in that email to confirm that they still want to subscribe to your email service and that they understand what they are signing up for.

Basically, the Double Opt-In makes your subscriber list more targeted and to a large degree 'weeds out' those who are not really interested in receiving future emails from you.

The theory is that this should lead to less unsubscribers and significantly less people accusing you of SPAM. Providing that your actual follow-up emails are relevant of course!

Email Opt-Out

Again, this is automatically setup for you if you use one of the big email marketing service providers but let me explain why it's so important?

It follows that the Opt-out is the opposite of the Opt-in but it reinforces the same idea about SPAM.

The Opt-out is basically an 'Unsubscribe' link which is normally placed at the bottom of your emails and gives the subscriber the option to be removed from your email list.

Having a subscriber who is not interested in your emails is a complete waste of time.

Also, email marketing services have different ways of taking money from you but one of the most common is a subscriber threshold payment.

When you go beyond that threshold, for example more than 500 subscribers, you'll pay a bit more for the email marketing service.

So the first point here is that you are essentially paying for someone who is never going to be interested in what you're saying or will never buy from you.

Secondly, if you don't have an Opt-out (Unsubscribe) link then you are not meeting the CANSPAM guideline which is not a good place to be for a growing business.

Thirdly, you significantly increase your chances of being accused of SPAM if you don't provide your 'unhappy' subscriber with a way out.

And even for someone who is really interested in your email content it gives them extra confidence in your professional outlook when they see that Unsubscribe link at the end of the email.

Bottom line, its good business practise. As a final thought, and this goes with all links of course, do a test and make sure the link works!

Autoresponders

Advantages?

Some obvious, others not so much! Let's take a look at the advantages of using an Autoresponder (or email marketing service)?

Automated Mailing

Using an Autoresponder puts your email marketing campaign on autopilot.

You can pre-write your emails and schedule them to be sent to your subscribers at intervals to suit your campaign. This is relatively easy when you use the services of someone like Aweber and such a company should have good videos, user guides or a 'wizard' to show you how to do this.

Top Tip:

If you haven't yet decided on which email marketing service to use then it's a great idea to see what kind of support and help they offer for new users.

Make sure the service is right for you!

Automated mailing allows you to plan your email campaign a long time before you get that first subscriber.

Let me give you an example:

One of my email campaigns was written primarily around the subject of getting traffic to a website. Obviously I wanted subscribers to my list to be interested in 'creating more traffic'.

So the Lead Magnet I used for the subscription form on my blog was also about Traffic Generation.

To tie everything in nicely, I also released a few articles which were about 'How to Attract Traffic' as well!

So you can see, this Automated Mailing service allowed me to have a good think about the whole package that I was offering to my visitors. With so much information about Traffic Generation being fed to my visitors, I was sure that the majority of people who signed up for my mailing list would appreciate the information that I was going to send them.

Back to having your business on Autopilot!

I've always thought that your most valuable commodity with a business is time! Sure, money is important but all money really does is help us create more time (think outsourcing etc.).

With a good autoresponder, detailed planning and a bit of hard work at the beginning, you create time for yourself further down the line.

As you get better at this you will start to plan further and further ahead and before you know it your business will be able to run on autopilot whilst you enjoy that holiday in the sun or relax at Christmas time.

This is where Autoresponders really come into their own. They create time and give you freedom!

Aweber

I use Aweber and have for a number of years but I'm very aware that other people prefer MailChimp whilst others swear by GetResponse etc. and the list could go on!

If you look online at some of the Internet Marketing Forums, like Warrior or Elance, you'll see that opinion really is divided between which one is the best.

The main ones all seem to have similar functionality but it really boils down to personal preference, which payment plan suits you best and which interface you are most comfortable working with.

Personally, I hate spending too long getting used to any software or service (talking about time again!) and the training tutorials that Aweber provide seem to be simple enough even for me to follow!

Also, with Aweber, the user interface is very friendly and most people won't find it difficult or particularly time consuming to setup an email campaign.

The pricing with Aweber is also very competitive and you pay a monthly fee as opposed to a 'pay as you go' type of service. $19/month (correct at time of writing) is what you pay for up to 500 subscribers and there is a subscriber tier system after that amount.

When I first started looking for an Autoresponder service I was a bit unsure on whether this monthly amount represented good value for money but believe me, when you start using the service and build up your subscriber list, all on autopilot, the value becomes very clear.

Alternative Services

I've included a list of some of the other main email marketing services which are available below. I can't personally vouch for the quality of all these alternatives and would advise you to do your own research before entering into a contract with any such service.

You might find that these services offer a discounted trial period so at least you'll be able to try before you buy!

GetResponse

Mail Chimp

Benchmark

iContact

Your Autoresponder Sequence

A few thoughts on the frequency of delivering emails to your subscribers.

This may depend on your particular niche or the demographic of your subscriber but as a rule, I would aim to pre-plan an email campaign to last for at least 30 days.

There's nothing stopping you increasing this as you go along but it makes real sense to give yourself some breathing room in case circumstances change and you're unable to write new emails for a few weeks.

The last thing you want is to lose your subscribers because you forgot to email them and they in turn forgot who you were! Also, at a minimum, you need to be emailing your subscribers at least once a week; preferably more (think every 3/4 days).

Email Marketing Informer

This is a balance between bombarding them daily and making them fed up with your emails and not emailing them enough and they end up not recognising your email address (and thinking you're SPAM).

MODULE 6 – TRAFFIC

This Module will be looking at the two types of traffic, Free and Paid.

Personally I've got more experience with free traffic and the majority of visitors to my site and therefore the vast majority of my subscribers have come from this kind of traffic.

Because this guide is built around my experiences and about what has worked for me, you'll find more information in this module about free traffic than the paid alternatives. Where possible however, I will try and point you in the right direction with the paid methods.

Free Traffic

Most of my free traffic has come from good quality (and targeted) information articles. To make these articles of the right 'quality' however, I've learnt to follow a few methods which make my content targeted, optimised and ready to drive the maximum number of visitors possible to my site.

So, for the first part of this module I'm going to explain how I make my articles rank, so they can drive 'targeted' traffic to my site and help me turn visitors into interested subscribers to my email list.

The first thing we need to with pretty much any content online, if you want it to rank highly in the search engines (Google!), is to carry out some keyword research.

Let's use an example. I have a website called 'Easy Outdoor Living', a site which has information articles and product reviews on a wide range of outside living furniture. I also have an email capture form on this site which has a Lead Magnet, in this case a guide to holding the perfect BBQ party, and I want to drive some targeted traffic to this Lead Magnet and start collecting subscribers for an email campaign.

To do this, I am going to write some articles which will target the right sort of visitors for my email campaign and will hopefully rank highly in the search engines for specific keywords.

Google Keyword Planner

Now using the Google Keyword Planner is a book pretty much in itself and I'm not going to tackle it here. However, take a look at the following guide which will give you a good headstart in getting to grips with this great tool:

http://searchengineland.com/how-to-use-the-keyword-planner-the-new-keyword-tool-from-google-adwords-157123

Another good way to learn about the Google Keyword Planner is from Google themselves and they have some useful guides which you can use to get use to their interface. A good place to start:

https://support.google.com/adwords/answer/2999770?hl=en

Market Samurai

Another way I do keyword research is to use some software called 'Market Samurai' which gives you a great insight into keyword competition, lists alternative keywords, shows you which sites are ranking on the first page of Google for this keyword and how competitive those sites are.

It does a lot more than that as well but a full walkthrough is not within the scope of this guide. However if you want to check out what Market Samurai can do first hand then check them out here:

http://www.emailmarketinginformer.com/recommends-Market-Samurai

You might ask why you would want to bother with software such as Market Samurai when the Google Keyword Planner is free to use?

Good question and it all boils down to one thing again, time!

I still use Google Keyword Planner to do a quick 'wet finger in the air' and to see if a keyword looks good to work with but you then need to evaluate the competition for that keyword and find out how difficult that keyword is going to be to rank on page 1 of Google.

When you start using Market Samurai, you'll realise that keywords you thought looked profitable and seemed to have low competition, are in fact going to be very difficult to rank for in the top page of Google.

Short answer, Market Samurai will give you the 'big picture' on that keyword and should help in not wasting time on keywords that you will never rank well for.

SEO (Search Engine Optimization)

By choosing the right keyword for your article, you have already started with your SEO but now you need to optimize in other ways:

1.   Make sure your keyword is used in the URL (web address) for the article. For example, the following URL is an example from a website of mine which does reviews on Outdoor Living products, in this case, a review on the Web Spirit Gas Grill:

http://www.easyoutdoorliving.com/weber-spirit-gas-grill/

2.   Your keyword should be included in the body text of your article but you don't want to 'stuff' your content full of it!

You'll find a ton of advice online about different percentages to aim for but I've never worried about the density of keywords (how many times it appears in an article compared with the size of the article itself) and I've had no problem ranking articles well.

My advice here, and you'll see others advise the same, is to include your keyword in your article as much as possible whilst making your content look and read natural. No keyword stuffing at the expense of a good, readable piece of work!

3. As well as your main keyword, you also want to try and include some 'secondary' keywords in your article as well.

    For example, the keyword for my BBQ article is 'Beginners BBQ Guide'. Whilst doing my keyword research, I find that 'Easy BBQ Dinners' & 'BBQ Party DIY' are good secondary keywords to include in my article.

Again you shouldn't concern yourself with stuffing these keywords in, just fit them naturally if possible. If you can't include them then don't worry about it, better to have a good, readable article than one that just looks like it was produced by a robot for a robot!

SEO Plugins

Your keyword has more work to do but if you're using WordPress you can save time by using a 'free' WordPress Plugin called 'WordPress SEO'.

Also called 'WordPress SEO by Yoast', this plugin gives you full SEO control of your WordPress Page or Post from a simple interface which appears at the bottom of the article that you're writing in WordPress. Here's an example:

WordPress SEO by Yoast

General Page Analysis Advanced Social

Snippet Preview   ⑦   **Weber Spirit Gas Grill** -
www.easyoutdoorliving.com/weber-spirit-gas-grill/
Weber Spirit Gas Grill Review. Visit Easy Outdoor Living for full reviews on Gas Grills,
outdoor furniture and appliances and to find the best prices online

Focus Keyword: ⑦   Weber Spirit Gas Grill

Your focus keyword was found in:
• Article Heading: Yes (1)
• Page title: Yes (1)
• Page URL: Yes (1)
• Content: Yes (4)
• Meta description: Yes (1)

SEO Title: ⑦   Weber Spirit Gas Grill -

Meta Description: ⑦   Weber Spirit Gas Grill Review. Visit Easy Outdoor Living for full reviews on Gas Grills, outdoor furniture and appliances and to find the best prices online

The meta description will be limited to 156 chars, 0 chars left.

FIGURE 3 - WORDPRESS SEO BY YOAST

Link Building

This is another important part of the optimization of your article and includes both internal and external links.

Internal Links

These are placed as text links or in images (more on image optimization later) and have two main purposes:

1. To help your readers navigate a bit more easily and give them more 'incentive' to stay on your site a bit longer.

   The navigation aspect of this is quite straight-forward. By placing appropriate internal links within your article your reader is able to navigate to this information a lot more quickly than searching through your menus or typing into a 'search box'. It makes your site more user friendly!

   Having these text links also encourages your visitor to stay on your site longer and not 'click-away'. If you haven't heard of a phrase called 'Bounce Rate', then this is the rate at which visitors arrive at your site only to quickly leave and go somewhere else!

How quickly and frequently visitors do this is used by the search engines, and Google in particular, in evaluating the content and relevance of your site. In general, the lower the bounce rate, the more credibility the search engines will give to your work, which should lead to increased rankings.

2. To help the Search Engine 'Spiders' navigate through your site, find as much content as possible and get all your pages indexed and ranked. The Search Engine Spiders are the internet robots that go hunting for website content. It certainly won't hurt your chances of getting ranked if you point them in the right direction!

External Links

As with Internal Links, you can add External Links to both your text and images and used correctly, these are great for SEO.

These links have three main purposes:

1. They are quite commonly used for affiliate links and are most effective when they are used in context with the information surrounding them, or a 'latest deal' which is guaranteed to grab the attention of the reader.

2. They can also be used to assist your reader with finding out more information from other sources. For example, my article on the 'Beginners BBQ Guide' talks about options for marinating your meat! I would include a link or two here which could help the reader get more information about marinating and cooking if they wanted to do so.

3. But possibly the main reason for having these External Links is to demonstrate to the Search Engines that your site is not a lonely

beast just trying to make money out of unsuspecting web surfers! By including good quality External Links in your content you are proving (or at least playing the game?) that you want your visitor to get the most information from your site as possible and that you're not afraid to be a part of the bigger world-wide community.

Google happens to like this.

Note on External Links:

It's probably not a good idea to overcrowd your content with External Links but it is a very good idea to include them where possible.

However, always make sure that with any linking (and this includes images) you enable the 'open in new window' option. You want to give your reader the best experience possible but you don't want to lose them straight away to another website and by opening this link in a new window, your site will still be visible in the previous window.

Note on Affiliate Links

Using the example of the 'Easy Outdoor Living' site, this website has Amazon Affiliate links in the text and also in the images.

Now there is some debate on this subject but in my experience with using affiliate links, you don't want the search engines to see good quality content that have multiple links going to Amazon (for example). Coincidence or not, I've experienced sites getting 'slapped down' because there's too many links going to one place.

What you can do however is use a WordPress Plugin called 'Pretty Links' which lets you take the affiliate link and create your own based on your websites address.

It looks better, it helps with SEO and it also keeps your entire link collection in one handy area.

Affiliate Program Terms & Conditions

Always follow the Terms & Conditions of the main Affiliate Program. In the example of Amazon, they require that your visitors need to know where they will be going when they click on a link. This is quite easy to do though and you can just add a suitable sentence to the link title attribute, such as "Click HERE to find the Best Deals on BBQ's at Amazon now..."

Images

Images are quite often forgotten about in articles and it wouldn't take you long to find a picture in an article which has no link attached to it or hasn't been optimized correctly to help with the SEO for that article.

We previously talked about the WordPress SEO (by Yoast) Plugin and this excellent add-on will certainly remind you when your images aren't optimized!

Essentially, you need to include your main keyword (or one of your secondary keywords, if you have multiple images) in the 'image title attribute' and the 'Alt Tag'. You also need to make sure that the file name for that image corresponds with the keyword that you're trying to rank for and that if you want to link with the image, make sure again that the link opens in a new window, emphasis here on keeping your site on your visitors screen!

Guest Blogging

Another great way to get free traffic is to 'Guest Blog' on sites that already have a good amount of traffic arriving at their site. You need to make your content good, relevant and acceptable to the owner of that website but you can potentially tap into a lot of targeted traffic by doing this.

Finding Sites to Accept Guest Posts

Instead of spending fruitless hours looking for suitable site owners to approach, and again we're trying to save time here, how about having a look at ezinearticles (http://ezinearticles.com/) and then doing the following:

1.   Find articles on topics which are similar to what you're talking about!
2.   Try and makes sure that the article meets your standard of writing! Do they read right? Would you want to include your content on a site that has such articles?
3.   Look for the writers' site details in the articles 'About the Author' section. Go and visit the site.
4.   Make contact with the Author and enquire about swapping articles between sites or making a guest post!

That's it! It still takes a bit of time and patience but it gives you a headstart over just typing into Google and sifting through the results for suitable blogs to guest post on.

Forums

The final free traffic solution that I'm going to share here is Forums!

The two sites that I recommend for free traffic generation are Warrior Forum and Elance. Sites like 'The Warrior Forum' are great for getting free traffic providing you do the following:

1.   Sort out your signature, from day one! Your signature is what appears at the bottom of your forum posts and it gives readers of the forum a chance to visit your own personal site (or offer) if they've found you interesting in the forum and they want to find out more about what you're about?

This signature doesn't have to be anything fancy and sometimes 'simple' can be the way to go but make sure that whenever you post, there is an external link nearby that visitors can follow for 'more information'.

Thanked 18 Times in 14 Posts   "Build a Fantastic Traffic Generating Blog Today"

Get Your FREE Bloggers Roadmap Report @ The Jon Crimes 'Easy Internet Marketing' Blog

Edit   Quote   Multiquote   Quick Reply

FIGURE 4 - FORUM SIGNATURE

2.   Become a resident expert!

Apart from 'selling' the link in your signature, you're also trying to build up a web presence with your forum posts and it's essential that you make a positive contribution to that forum. Look on the forum for topics which interest you and that you have some knowledge in. Post against these threads and people will soon see you as one of the 'experts'.

3.   Don't argue on the forum. It definitely goes on but if you want to be professional then don't get involved with this sort of thing.

A simple 'we'll have to agree to disagree' or 'I respect your opinion however.. .' is probably a better way to deal with arguments online. Don't forget, even one bad comment can destroy reputations online, don't get suckered in!

There is of course many other ways to get free targeted traffic to your site to increase your email subscriber list but I've shared with you the 3 methods which have really worked for me.

Over the past few years I've found that it's important to channel your efforts into a few things that work as opposed to many things that end up getting you nowhere. If any of these methods work for you, there's no reason why you shouldn't stick with them.

Paid Traffic

As I said in the introduction, I haven't really used paid traffic methods to drive visitors to my site and in all honesty, I haven't needed to but what I will do is give you a brief summary of a few methods which you can follow up with your own research if necessary.

Adwords

Google Adwords is one of the most popular forms of paid advertising on the internet and you could spend many an hour reading about the tips and tricks on how to make the most of this service.

In case you haven't come across Adwords before, these adverts are what you see on the right hand side of your Google Search screen whenever you do a search for a particular keyword. Whereas, the results on the left are called the 'Organic' search and you 'control' your position here with SEO!

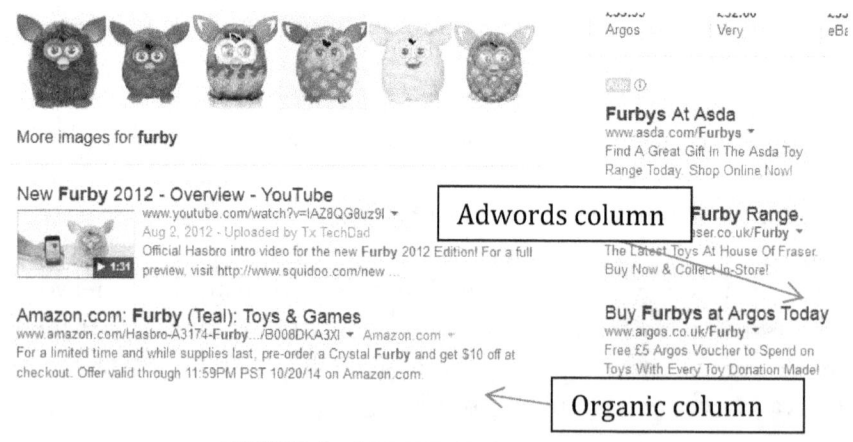

FIGURE 5 - GOOGLE ADVERTISING

Essentially, people 'bid' on these keywords and the winners get positioned on the right hand side of the screen in order of where they came in the bidding process. It stands to reason that the more popular the keyword, the more money the winning bidders will have to pay.

If you want to find out more about Adwords, then I've been told that the following book comes highly recommended, it's also worth checking out some of the 100+ reviews for this book as well, Perry Marshall certainly knows his stuff!

Ultimate Guide to Google AdWords: How to Access 100 Million People in 10 Minutes

Ezine Advertising

Ezines are online newsletters which are used to share news, website promotions and updates with interested readers.

With Ezine advertising you place an ad for your site in these Ezines and providing you do it right, choose the right Ezines for your niche etc., you should be able to generate good traffic to your site.

I've got to be honest, I haven't tried this but I know of others who have and still swear by it as a good traffic generator.

I also thought that this method of traffic generation was good in 2007 but not so good some 8 years later! However, a quick search on 'Ezine Advertising' in Google gives me a strong impression that a lot of people are still using it today and it is working for them!

Might be worth some further research?

Solo Ads

Solo Ads are an agreement between two internet marketers and consists of one marketer sending out an email to their list on behalf of the other marketer.

This is usually a one-time email and there are no other offers included in this email, just the offer/site details from the marketer requesting the Solo Ad.

Solo Ads have been around for a while but I've noticed they have become extremely popular recently with more and more marketers promoting offers and building their subscriber base by getting others to mail their list.

Also, when you get a marketer to mail his list with your offer, they are basically 'endorsing' you and that alone can prove to be very valuable.

Solo Ads are great for building your email list very quickly but if your end-game is to promote high-end offers then you might need to think twice about whether this form of advertising is suitable for your needs!

A lot of marketers will have big lists full of subscribers who love free stuff (and who doesn't?). If you try and promote a $200 affiliate offer to this list then your conversion rates are not going to be that great! Solo Ads work well when you're promoting lower priced offers and freebies which can then lead onto the bigger offers.

Want to know more about Solo Ads?

You're in luck!
This is the one area of paid advertising that I've used, quite a lot!

I've even created a guide which can help you make the most out of this advertising method. Link below:

www.emailmarketinginformer.com/solo-ads

Facebook Advertising

Advertising on Facebook seems to be getting more and more popular but not having used this form of paid advertising yet, and from reading about other people's experiences with it, I'm not wholly convinced that it is suitable for my needs as an Internet Marketer?

Saying that, the information that Facebook collects from its users might be very useful when you need to target specific people and their demographics to build effective advertising campaigns!

I've found a great guide if you want to find out more for yourself and again, don't be put off with the '600 Million Customers in 10 Minutes' bit, this is a great guide to Advertising with Facebook:

www.EmailMarketingInformer.com/recommends-ultimate-facebook-advertising

MODULE 7 – KEEPING SUBSCRIBERS

Start from the very beginning!

You've built a site that is attracting good traffic, your Lead Magnet is appropriate to your site and to the majority of the visitors that are going to see your content and you've started to get subscribers to your list.

So how do you make sure that you keep those 'VIP's'?

There's no real shortcuts here I'm afraid but it's not that difficult. What you need to do is simply treat your subscribers how you would like to be treated and make sure you hold their hand, especially at the very beginning!

The Thank You

The hard part is getting people to subscribe to your list in the first place but if you carry out what we've discussed in this guide and do things right
from the start then those subscribers will come.

When they do, make sure they get a big *Thank You* for subscribing to your list. A few thoughts on this:

1. With the big Autoresponder services like Aweber, you are able to customise the 'Thank You' page and you have a choice whether to do this with text or, in Awebers case, you can use a Video 'Thank You' as well.

    I personally go for the text 'Thank You'!

2. Again, with the more popular Autoresponder services this is already covered, but you need to make sure that your subscriber is reminded that they need to carry out the 'Double Opt-in' before they start receiving emails from you.

3. When they click on the 'Opt-in' that appears in their email account they are now fully subscribed to your list and you can begin to send them emails.

    For the first email, Thank them again and explain what the format of future emails will be, how you appreciate their feedback, explain that they can 'Opt-out' at any point and let them know that you will be including more great 'free' information during the following email series.

It really is important to build a great relationship with your list from day 1.

Get Whitelisted

A useful trick that I learnt a while ago was to get yourself whitelisted by your list at the earliest opportunity.

By getting 'Whitelisted' I mean being added to their 'safe sender' list. If you do this early then there's virtually no chance of your email getting lost in their Junk email folder. Face it, if your email ends up in there, then there was probably no point in sending it anyway?

I aim to get my subscriber to add me to their safe sender list by adding the follow words into the first email that I send them (this can be the first email in your Autoreponder series):

"I'll be sending some great information to you about (add your subject here) over the next few weeks as well as some exclusive content which no one else will see!

To make sure that you don't miss out and that these emails go into Junk folder by mistake, please carry out the following:

Add my Email address to your 'Whitelist'. Sometimes known as the 'Safe Sender' List.

I've included some 'quick' guides below which will help you do this, very fast. Please choose the guide which is appropriate to your email service provider or have a look at their 'Help' files:

If you get any problems with this, please let me know.

Thanks, Jon"

A good guide to include with this email is called "How to Whitelist an Email Address". I've included the link to this below:

www.meetingmade.com/Whitelisting.aspx

NOW GRANTED THIS ISN'T GOING TO WORK FOR EVERYONE BUT YOU'LL BE AMAZED AT THE AMOUNT OF PEOPLE WHO WILL ACTUALLY TAKE THE TIME TO DO THIS WHEN THERE'S A CHANCE THEY'LL MISS OUT ON FREE GOODIES IF THEY DON'T!

OF COURSE, IF YOU PROMISE SOME EXCLUSIVE CONTENT THEN YOU NEED TO FOLLOW UP WITH THAT PROMISE AND WHAT I TRY TO DO IS HAVE A SMALL EBOOK OR REPORT WHICH I CAN SEND TO MY LIST A WEEK OR SO AFTER THE EMAIL SERIES STARTS.

It's entirely up to you when you do this but it's important to do so whilst the memory of that promise is still fresh in their minds, I would suggest no more 2 weeks after that second email.

Who's opening their email?

Depending on what type of email campaign you have running, it is usually a good idea to separate the 'action takers' from those or who aren't quite so active!

When your list grows in size then you don't want to waste time promoting to subscribers who are not interested in making such a purchase, however, you don't want to remove these people altogether.

How about creating another list which offers more generalised information and the occasional affiliate link which might be more to their likening?

For the 'action takers', those who appear to have a genuine interest in your list and consistently open the emails, and possibly even click through to your promotions, then these subscribers really are your tier 1 people and deserve to be treated as such.

Analytics

So how do you find out who's opening their emails and in general who your subscribers really are?

We use analytics.

The larger email marketing providers will have their own built in Analytic programs and you should refer to your chosen provider for more details.

What analytics can do for us however is pretty much standard across all the providers.

Geography

You can start to get a feel for your subscribers even with something as simple as their geography! The country they come from can have a direct relationship to how they approach the information in your emails and whether or not they would be interested in clicking through to one of your 'promotional' links.

A person's location in the world also helps with deciding when you should send your emails out. For instance, if you're based in the United Kingdom but the bulk of your subscribers are in the United States, then you really wouldn't want to send your emails at 8 AM UK time.

Your subscribers would be receiving these emails at 4 AM or even earlier!

If your list contains large groups of subscribers from different time zones then you might want to group those different time zones together and have a separate list for each with email delivery times to suit!

Demographics

Finding out about the age, gender and location (back to geography again!) of your subscribers can make a huge difference to how well your emails are received.

But how do you do this?

How you accomplish this depends on which email marketing service you use, whether you want to pay for additional email analytical services and to what degree you want to analyse your subscribers.

Here are some options for you which you can obviously use to suit your circumstances:

1. Take a look at your subscribers IP address. By doing this you will be able to separate your list based on their locations and in some cases this should also give you an idea about their potential buying power.

    You can discover locations by IP addresses by using the following site:

    www.iplocation.net/

2. Feeling brave? How about using your initial signup form a bit more than just "Name & Email please?"

This can be great for giving you detailed information on the demographics of your subscribers but I would also add that your site content, Lead Magnet and their impulse to sign up for your emails needs to be very strong.

3.   Consolidate! So you have a list of subscribers but haven't really got to know them properly yet! How about setting up a survey where you can collect information on your 'customers' in exchange for something valuable to them of course.

4.   You could offer a free gift (think report, exclusive content or eBook) in exchange for their time and/or have a prize lucky dip where some lucky subscriber to your survey gets a superb top of the range gadget.

In this survey you can ask for more information about themselves, what they like about your site/emails, how you can improve the content you send to them, how much they would be willing to spend to become successful online (change to suit your niche) etc. Whatever you ask them, you need to make it worthy of their time and your expense.

The last point there about asking how much they would be willing to spend is a very important one as this is used to gauge their buying power!

Review your content!

Your list and the content you supply to your subscribers should be seen as a sort of 'living beast'!

What you need to do is carry out a review of your email content, have a good look at who the main bulk of your subscribers are (back to demographics) and adapt your emails accordingly.

A few questions to ask yourself:

1. Is your content still relevant?

2. Are you getting feedback from your subscribers? This can be from surveys you've sent them, subscribers sending you questions or more drastically, large numbers of unsubscriptions! The trick is to recognise these trends and to take the necessary action.

    Again, this all boils down to getting the website traffic - site content - lead magnet formula - email content right. If there's a mismatch then there's a good chance that subscribers will be unhappy with the service and might vote with their feet.

3. Don't forget, your list is just that, a list of email addresses. What you feed to that list is the important thing and that has got to be as close a match as possible to your list's expectations. If you start to get the sort of feedback that says otherwise then you need to re-evaluate subscriber expectations again.

Customer Incentives

So how do you keep your subscribers engaged enough and happy to remain on your list? A few thoughts:

1. Give them continued value. The last thing you want to do is to catch the right traffic, have a great lead magnet, start sending them excellent informative emails that they can easily attach great value to, only to reduce the quality of that content after the initial 'big push'.

    This is guaranteed to get your subscribers questioning their loyalty to you and before long they'll be unsubscribing. Consistent good quality content is the key here.

2. Create and develop loyalty. You really need to make your subscribers feel wanted and there are a number of ways to do this.

How about creating 'exclusive' bonuses, just for them. Make sure these are not available anywhere else, not on your site or offered as part of a lead magnet and let your subscribers settle into your email series before offering such a bonus.

I find that waiting until they've received at least 10 emails and then include a *bonus* in number 11 along with a 'thank you' for their continued loyalty.

3. The 11th email! You could also use this email (please use any number to suit your campaign if '11' isn't suitable!) to let them know that they are now included in your very popular 'loyalty program' which will give them first viewing of upcoming products, promotions and offer great special deals, *only available to them*.

But above all, make them feel valued and don't forget that you have to exchange something with them in return for their continued loyalty to you.

The Special List

So you have subscribers who are especially active on your list? Why not put them on a special list that goes that little bit further to nurture more loyalty? Examples with this could include offering them a truly exceptional discount on your latest (next?) product or promotion.

If you sell physical products through your list, how about giving them an exclusive discount code which can be used on their next purchase or if you promote other peoples offers, try and negotiate a special deal with the vendor and offer this to the best buyers as a special thank you.

If you treat your subscriber's right, they'll most probably stick by you. As a bonus from them to you, they might even recommend your site (and therefore list) to friends and family, win-win.

MODULE 8 – ADVANCED EMAIL MARKETING

Broadcasting emails

No matter how good your autoresponder email series is, you'll find yourself sending out broadcast emails to your subscribers more frequently as your list grows.

A broadcast is an email which is sent to your entire list at the same time.

This is separate from your 'autoresponder sequence' but can still be scheduled in advance. They are great for newsletters, short-notice product offers or any material which needs frequent updates.

Important:

Its worth noting that some email marketing services will not update (add or remove to an email list) whilst a broadcast is in progress and this can include the scheduled 'delay'. Check to see how your provider deals with email broadcasting.

The Swipe File

If you're the sort of person who never runs out of good quality things to say and you can remember how to get the most from your email content, time after time, then good luck to you!

For the rest of us, a 'Swipe File' is an excellent way to generate effective emails for your new or continuing campaign, and quickly.

A swipe file is essentially a collection of content, headers, calls to action etc. which you can literally 'swipe', copy and paste into your new email or document. For email marketing, I tend to keep my swipe files in a spreadsheet format but you could quite easily just have long MS Word (or similar) document with all your email 'swipes' listed in it.

When you come to write a new email or add an email to your existing campaign, your swipe file is useful to:

1. Add content direct from your swipe file into the new message, changing important details like product names, date information etc.

2. Act as a reminder about how you want your email message to be laid out! Sometimes, you will need a 'memory jog' when writing and this is especially the case when writing new emails for your campaign.

A/B Split Testing

How do you really know which email sequence, campaign or special offer is giving you the best return for that most valuable of things, your time?
You need to Test!

There's no big secret with A/B Split Testing, it just means that you are testing version A against version B for effectiveness and optimization. With email marketing, you can do this by creating two segments within your list and then comparing one against the other.

Again, the bigger email marketing services, like Aweber, make this quite easy to do and by following their tutorials you will be up and running very quickly.

So what should you Split Test?

You could of course split test pretty much everything but I would recommend that you stick with 3 sections of your campaign.

The email capture form

You know you're attracting visitors to your website but you're not happy with how many people are subscribing to your email list. You need to split test your email capture form, making sure that your Lead Magnet is suitable, your wording in your capture form grabs attention and that it is placed appropriately on your webpage.

When your capture form is performing, you then need to pay attention to the emails in your list:

The Subject Line.

Very obvious when you think about it but quite often forgotten about in favour of the main content of the email!

Your subject line is the first door your subscriber needs to open to go on and read your email. If it doesn't grab their attention, the wording is wrong or it's pitched to the wrong audience, then that's all your email will ever be, a subject line.

Until it gets put in the trash of course!

This is a great place to start with your testing. The subject line you think is good becomes version A and an alternative, maybe worded slightly differently, with a different tone or attention grabber becomes version B. Do the test, see how they compare and if version B does better that A, then use that version in future emails.

Is your new version getting the results you want? If not, repeat the test with a new version B until you're happy with the results.

The Main Body

Same principle as with the subject line but this time you're focusing on the main body of text within your email message.

If you're happy that your emails are getting opened but there's a lack of subscriber action from the main text (assuming you have such an action!) then you need to test an alternative message against this one.

Being a book about marketing I should at least mention the AIDA acronym once! AIDA stands for Attention, Interest, Desire and Action.

These are the exact things you need to install in your subscriber from your email message and after a good attention grabbing subject line, it's good practise to grab that attention again and develop the interest in your product/offer etc.

You can then outline the advantages and benefits (as opposed to features!), create Desire for that product and tell your subscriber that it will satisfy their needs and finally 'encourage' them to take that all important action, through a link or similar.

Your P.S's

The P.S is becoming extremely popular in emails as a useful marketing tool. You've probably seen these a lot in emails that you've received as a subscriber and they're certainly very effective in turning a doubting subscriber into a curious, why not have a look, type of person!

The P.S or Postscript, literally means *"writing which is added after the main body of a text"* in the form of a small message just after the writer's signature. These are ideal to reinforce the AIDA principle that we talked about above and are commonly used to reiterate the benefits of a product or service as well as highlighting the need to take action 'now'.

The P.S is great when used as a very brief summary of what was in the main text and it is not unknown for someone to read the majority of the email, too quickly, not take the information in but then become interested by the Postscripts at the bottom and decide to give the content another go.

When I say Postscripts, yes you can have more than one!

In fact the other day I received an email which included P.S, P.P.S and P.P.P.S after the signature! All contained a brief summary which reinforced various aspects of the AIDA part of the message and gave the email a lot more weight.

Personally though, 3 of these would be my maximum, you don't want your Postscripts to rival the main body of your email in terms of size!

Automated Rules

With Automated Rules you can manage subscribers on more than one list simultaneously.

For example, you have more than one email list, this might be hard to imagine now but it's amazing how things develop once you get your first list moving!

You also have a weekly newsletter that you want to send to multiple lists, one list might be for potential buyers, another list for established customers etc.

Then probably the most effective way of achieving this is by using automated rules.

You'll find that most of the bigger email marketing services (like Aweber) have this function built into their service and you might find that the way they work is slightly different depending on what service you use!

As always, refer to your provider for help if you're not sure how to use this function.

With Aweber, you select the lists to move your subscribers around to and then basically the rules take care of the 'grunt' work. You can add them to as many lists as you like or unsubscribe them as appropriate.

Some of the rules that Aweber have include:

Subscribe-on-subscribe

For this rule you have multiple lists and when a visitor subscribes to one list then they are automatically subscribed to another list as well. I've found this to be very useful when you have two lists which do different things.

For example, one list is primarily just an information list, full of useful hints and tips and which is emailed to subscribers on a fairly frequent basis (every 3 or 4 days). The second list is more of a 'selling list' which is aiming to turn the subscriber into a buyer.

My preference with this list is to be slightly less frequent than the first list and initially I would test this list to deliver an email every 7 days. At least then my subscribers would be getting two quality information emails for the price of one 'selling' email!

Unsubscribe-on-subscribe

Depending on your website and business model, you might have reason to take a 'customer' off a particular list when they subscribe to another list. A good example of this is when they buy from you and therefore become an established customer.

Whereas before they were receiving emails which were trying to convert them into customers, that goal has now been achieved! In the process of making this purchase, you can subscribe them to a new 'customer only' list and remove them from the original prospector list.

Unsubscribe-on-unsubscribe

I personally find this rule vital in meeting CANSPAM guidelines and in avoiding SPAM complaints from subscribers who have made their intentions very clear that they no longer want to be on your list (or lists!). So when someone clicks the unsubscribe link at the bottom of your email, they are automatically unsubscribed from all your lists.

The last thing you want is to have someone unsubscribe from one list and then receive emails from the other lists, forget what they unsubscribed to and then start complaining to your email marketing provider that you are spamming them!

Bottom line, if they want to unsubscribe, let them and make sure they are unsubscribed completely.

There's a lot more to Automated Rules than the brief summary I've given but what's on offer very much depends on what email service you use. If you already use an email marketing provider but don't use automated rules then take a look at their help files or training videos to see exactly what they have to offer.

Create a Segment

It makes real sense to pay special attention to subscribers who have already made a purchase from you or taken that 'action'.

You can do this by segmenting customers.

By segmenting 'proven' customers you can reach out to them and offer them the type of benefits that they'll find hard to refuse, increasing your sales in the process.

With segmenting you can:

1. Reward your loyal customer with discounts and specials which make them feel more appreciated and more likely to stick around!

2. Create new business! Think about, if your customer is that happy with your service and think that you're going the extra mile, just for them, then there's a good chance they're not going to keep quiet about it. New business will almost certainly come your way.

3. Even without these tactics, the fact that you've segmented proven customers together means that this group is more likely to purchase in the future.

So how do you Segment Customers?

My example is with Aweber again but other email marketing services have similar functionality.

With Aweber you install a script on your website called 'Email Web Analytics' and then use either 'Web Page Tracking' or 'Goal Tracking' to analyse your subscribers to start segmenting customers. The actual 'segmenting' of your customers is done automatically by this script. All you need to do is select the actual criteria.

Web page tracking

With web page tracking, you can select a webpage that you want to segment subscribers against. So if your selected webpage is the 'Thanks for Payment' page, then you can instruct the script (in the case of the Aweber script) to segment (or move!) those subscribers into their own special group.

Goal tracking

With goal tracking you select your criteria against set goals. For example, you could have an exclusive list for subscribers who have purchased more than $500 worth of products from your site. In this case you would set a financial goal of +$500 and any customers that meet that criteria would automatically be segmented into that special group.

Segmenting your list is a great way to organise your subscribers into special groups that require a 'different' sort of attention than your average subscriber. Checkout your provider and see what they have to offer.

Spam Filters - How to beat them?

Maybe that's a poor question!

It's probably better to think of Spam Filters as something you should aim to be compliant with as opposed to trying to beat them all the time.

If you play by the rules and treat your subscriber's right then you shouldn't get too many problems but I've included a few tips which should help to make your experience with Spam Filters a lot more pleasant?

1. Pick your words carefully! Filters are very much like human eyebrows really, say the wrong thing and you'll get 'that look'. Any words that hint at sexual content or offer something which on closer examination seems unobtainable should be avoided. For the latter, think 'Millionaire in week, guaranteed' or 'Congratulations, you've won this top prize', words like 'guarantee' or 'congratulations' might well raise a flag with the filter. For sexual content, good look with getting that accepted by any Spam Filter!

2. Now I'm very guilty of this and it's something I need to edit for, the exclamation mark! Use this too much in the title of an email or in the subject body and your email may well end up in the Trash.

3. Always remember to review your emails before sending or adding to an autoresponder series.

4. Contact information and the Unsubscribe link. Very important, not only to meet CANPAM guidelines but to prevent your email being stopped by the filters and it also gives your subscriber confidence that they are dealing with a professional person and that they have the opportunity to unsubscribe should they wish to.

5. Use a spam checker to identify Phishing. A standard inbox filter will look for URLs in your content (*http://* and *www.*). If the link destination and the link text don't match you'll be accused of phishing. It's as simple as that and easier to do than you might think.

6. Including an unsubscribe link along with your company contact information makes you look far more trustworthy in the eyes of the spam filters.

7. Test, test, test. Without a doubt testing is your best chance of beating spam filters and increasing your deliverability. This allows you to check your spam scores, identify formatting errors in various different inboxes and make changes before hitting send.

    Don't leave your marketing efforts to chance; you can never do too much testing!

CONCLUSION

Congratulations on getting to the end of this book.

I know it's been quite a long read but there was so much that I wanted to cover and it's also nice to cater for the different experience levels out there!

This isn't the end though.

Firstly, I've been doing email marketing for some time and I'm in a position to help others just starting out or anyone who has any extra questions, with anything!

If I don't know the answer straight away then I also have access to some fantastic Internet Marketers who might well be able to point us all in the right direction.

Please don't hesitate to get in touch: Jon@joncrimes.com

There's also some bonus material that I've include in the next few pages, stuff which I really wish I had access to a few years ago.

There's a list of my Recommended Services, a Glossary of some of the common terms used in this 'game' and a Special Bonus! An Email Autoresponder series which you can use directly in your campaigns or just to take ideas from.

Please remember to change any product details (products come and go!) and insert your own affiliate links.

Speaking of links, it's worth using a Wordpress Plugin like 'Pretty Links' (mentioned previously) to make affiliate links a bit more pretty but more importantly to have them organized all in one place.

That's all for now and I'd love to know what you think of this book and how you're getting on?

To your success.

Jon Crimes

Email Marketing Informer

P.S. Don't forget to check out my Blog and sign up for the free email series!

P.P.S. You're going to LOVE the extra Special Bonus that you'll get for subscribing...

www.JonCrimes.com

RECOMMENDED SERVICES

Email Marketing Service Providers

Aweber

http://www.emailmarketinginformer.com/recommends-Aweber

GetResponse

http://www.emailmarketinginformer.com/recommends-GetResponse

Mail Chimp

http://mailchimp.com/

Benchmark

http://www.emailmarketinginformer.com/recommends-benchmark

iContact

https://www.icontact.com/

Internet Marketing Forums

Warrior Forum

http://www.warriorforum.com/

Elance

https://www.elance.com/

Keyword Research Tools

Google Keyword Planner

https://support.google.com/adwords/answer/2999770?hl=en

Email Marketing Informer

Market Samurai

http://www.emailmarketinginformer.com/recommends-Market-Samurai

WordPress

WordPress Guide

https://make.wordpress.org/support/user-manual/

InstaLegalPages (Wordpress Plugin)

http://instalegalpages.com/

SlickQuiz (WordPress Plugin)

https://wordpress.org/plugins/slickquiz/

Advertising

Google Adwords

http://www.emailmarketinginformer.com/recommends-Ultimate-Guide-Adwords

Solo Ads

http://www.emailmarketinginformer.com/recommends-Email-Solo-Ads

Facebook Advertising

http://www.emailmarketinginformer.com/recommends-Ultimate-Facebook-Advertising

Blog Building

Jon Crimes Internet Marketing Blog

http:www.joncrimes.com/blog

Bloggers Roadmap

http://www.bloggersroadmap.com/

iWriter

http://www.emailmarketinginformer.com/recommends-iWriter

Fiverr

https://www.fiverr.com/

Other Stuff!

Amazon Associate Program

http://www.emailmarketinginformer.com/Amazon-Associates-Guide

GFX-1

http://www.emailmarketinginformer.com/recommends-GFX-1

Google Keyword Planner

https://support.google.com/adwords/answer/2999770?hl=en

EzineArticles

http://ezinearticles.com/

IP Location Finder

http://www.iplocation.net/

GLOSSARY OF TERMS

A/B Split Testing – Testing with two variants, i.e. Email Message A and Email Message B.

Affiliate Marketing – Performance based marketing where a business rewards the Affiliate for each visitor/customer who visits/buys from that business.

Alt Tag – Text which is added to an image to assist search engine relevancy and site SEO.

Analytics – Tools used to analyse website performance in the search engines and to optimise SEO.

Autoresponder – Computer program/service which automatically answers emails sent to it.

Blog – A discussion or informational website, often subject specific, which consists of posts usually displayed in reverse chronological order.

Bounce Rate – The percentage of visitors who enter a site and then leave straight away without viewing other pages on the site.

CAN-SPAM - Controlling the Assault of Non-Solicited Pornography and Marketing. Guidelines for ethical email marketing.

CMS – Content Management System. A system which supports the collection, management and publishing of information, e.g. WordPress.

Demographics – The statistics of a given population.

Disclaimer - Any statement intended to specify or delimit the scope of rights and obligations that may be exercised and enforced by parties in a legally recognized relationship.

eBook – A book-length publication produced in digital form.

GKP – Google Keyword Planner. Free tool, provided by Google, which can help with choosing appropriate keywords.

Lead Magnet – Used to incentivise visitors to give their email in return for a subject related gift or offer.

IM – Internet Marketing. Advertising and marketing that uses the internet to drive sales.

IP Address – Internet Protocol Address. An address assigned to each device participating in a computer network.

Pop-up - Online advertising on the Internet intended to attract web traffic or capture email addresses.

P.S. – Postscript. Writing added after the main body of an email message.

SEO – Search Engine Optimisation. Process of affecting the visibility of a website or a web page in a search engine's paid or normal (organic) search.

Social Media - Social interaction among people in which they create, share or exchange information and ideas in virtual communities and networks.

Solo Ads - Solo Ads are email based advertising which is agreed between two parties to reach out to a list of subscribers that are registered to either.

Squeeze Page - A landing page created to obtain opt-in email addresses from prospective subscribers.

Swipe File - A collection of tested and proven advertising and sales emails.

URL – Uniform Resource Locator. The global address of documents and other resources on the Internet.

VIP – Very Important Person. Your visitor, subscriber or customer!

Whitelist – A list which that essentially says "those on the list will be accepted"! Get your subscribers whitelisted at the earliest opportunity.

WordPress – Content Management System software which allows you to create and manage websites.

Bonus

BONUS

AUTORESPONDER SEQUENCE

Disclaimer

The author will not be responsible for any losses or damages of any kind incurred by the reader whether directly or indirectly arising from the use of the information found in this eBook. No guarantees of income are made or implied. The reader assumes responsibility for use of information contained herein.

Introduction

Welcome to this Bonus, your free to use Autoresponder Sequence.

I've included this email autoresponder sequence for you to use directly in your email campaigns or to take some great ideas from and create your own campaigns based around your particular niche or subject area.

You can use the sequence directly or add some more informational emails to create more of a Hybrid email campaign.

These emails have been proven to make sales and keep subscribers engaged and happy on my email list but I must stress that this has also been backed up with many of the things we talked about in the main eBook, like having decent site content, a good Lead Magnet etc.

Think of these emails as an important part of your campaign but they are just that, a part of it!

More about the emails themselves:

This Bonus includes 35 emails.

You'll notice that the 'Take Action' at the bottom of the emails needs a 'Clickbank ID' adding to the link! (That should be your Clickbank ID of course).

I would also advise that you check the product and its link as you go through each email. Products do get removed from affiliate networks, such as Clickbank, from time to time, so make sure the offers are still valid!

New to Clickbank?

Don't worry, I've include a guide to using Clickbank, checkout this link below (it doesn't take long to get used to the Clickbank interface):

http://www.clickbankguide.com/

There's some great stuff through the above link by the way and with no hard sell! Enjoy and any problems please get in touch.

Jon

Jon@joncrimes.com

Day 0 – Introduction

SUBJECT: Thank You For Signing Up! Please Read...

Hi {!firstname_fix},

Thanks again for signing up to my newsletter.

My aim is to deliver great value and content to you so that you are not only educated in the field of internet marketing but are also well informed about products before you buy them.

There are so many people out there in the same boat as you, who have every intention of brining in a stable and consistent income online but very few are willing to pull the strings to make it happen.

You need to know that there are NO magic systems and that what you're trying to achieve online is a REAL business - not a side hobby. Let me assure you that if anyone does try to sell you a magic bullet, or 'blind sells' to you so that you don't know what you're getting it's more than likely too good to be true and wouldn't last in the long run.

My newsletter is all about informing you and making sure that you are aware of the methods that are available. From there you can decide which route you want to take and ultimately develop yourself.

There is no one way to make money online, and every marketer has their own style. Some like affiliate marketing, some like writing, some like using PPC, some like resell rights products, some like to create their own. You will eventually find yours and discover what you like doing the most!

So please stay tuned for my upcoming emails as I believe you will find that most valuable!

Day 1 – Free Killer Preseller

Hi {!firstname_fix},

There are stories all over the place about affiliate marketers living like kings just through their online sales. But, if you've tried to get in on that and you have found that it just isn't working for you, you've probably asked yourself what's going on.

Do you want to know the secret of how they're doing it?

If you're spending a fortune promoting affiliate products and you aren't seeing anything in return it's time to change the game plan. Let's face it; it just isn't as easy as it once was starting out as an affiliate marketer. We all know it.

Yet, at the same time there are a select few underground marketers who are not only making a profit with their affiliate sales, they are raking in an absolute fortune! So, what is it they know that you don't? That was the question I asked myself not that long ago. I knew there had to be something I was missing and I was right!

The make it or break it difference to succeeding online.

Here's the bottom line. It all comes down to the pre-sell. The mistake I was making, and I would be willing to bet you are too, is that I was trying to sell products. Wait a minute! Isn't that what you're supposed to do as an affiliate marketer?

Want to know something surprising?

The answer is no! If you want to really sell something, the answer is stop trying to sell it!

I know, sounds crazy, doesn't it? That's what I thought at first too until I put this system into play and found out what it could really do. And let me tell you, I was blown away! The simple truth is that people hate being forced into buying something. The real secret is learning how to pre-sell!

Sounds pretty simple, doesn't it?

Yet, it's probably one of the biggest problems that Internet marketers face today. In this business you need as much of a competitive edge as you can have. Pre-selling gives you the edge you need to not just grab people's interest but turn them into buyers!

What Aaron and the guys at KillerPreseller have done is they've already researched a product that sells, bought a copy of it, reviewed it inside out and then turned it into a landing-page.

Each landing page includes well written copy, a summary of the product at hand, a scoring system, and clean site graphics so you really don't have to do much work!

So not only are you getting the niche research done for you but you now know which product in which niche is profitable!

Grab your free affiliate templates below:

http://www.emailmarketinginformer.com/recommends/Killer-Preseller

P.S. There are real testimonials of people who have already had success with the free templates alone, but I'll give you a heads up that they've got an amazing upgrade if you want presentation videos on your site!

Day 2 – Instant Site Uploader

SUBJECT: A system with NO FTP'in, NO HTML, NO writing involved?...

We all need to use software at some point in our lives to be able to perform complicated tasks with relative ease.

Computer's need an operating system, graphic designers need Photoshop, writers need Microsoft Word, for online browsing you need FireFox etc.

The same is true in the world of internet marketing. New software sprouts up every day to make tedious and complicated tasks easy. Some do the job well, whilst some others still need improving.

There are lead generators that go out and collect emails for you. There are link builders that generate back links for you. There are article submitters that give your site more exposure.

But if you're a beginner, NONE of these tools will be any good to you because you won't know how to use them or get the most out of them.

However there is a new piece of online-based software on the market which allows beginners to select, edit and upload their own affiliate website within a matter of minutes.

No need to research a market
No need to pick affiliate products
No need to design your own website
No need to write any sales copy
No need to for an FTP uploader
No need to edit complicated HTML

And so much more…

They've really thought of everything… even video training so you know how to get traffic to your sites!

Not all of us were born with the gift of programming or creating beautiful mini-sites nor do we all have the time of day to learn all these picky details which is why Instant Site Uploader was created – for smart guys like us {!firstname_fix}.

Make no mistake about it, you need a nice site these days – not a newbie-looking site that no one would want to visit. Instant Site Uploader gives puts everything into one system to make your life easier so you can focus on promoting and making money.

See below what I mean here:
http://www.emailmarketinginformer.com/recommends/instant-site-uploader

Day 3 – Instant Site Uploader2

Hi {!firstname_fix},

If you read my email yesterday, you'll know that you can now use a single tool that allows you to get into the affiliate marketing game fast. And I mean fast.

It's an online-based piece of software called Instant Site Uploader and it's got EVERYTHING included to help you make money online.

I've already receive a couple of emails about this because it caused a bit of a stir, but let me try to answer a few of your questions...

Q. Are the websites downloadable and do I have to host it?

A. Yes you can download the websites. You must first upload them to your server and then you can download them to your PC. The system is mainly web-based to keep everything light and portable so even if you decide to work elsewhere you can log into the system and continue as normal and won't have to install any third party programs on your computer.

Q. How long will it really take for me to get a website up and running?

A. I've tried this system myself and once you've got your server ready and FTP details you can have a brand new site uploaded in less than 5 minutes. This is a lot quicker and more efficient than doing it manually.

Q. What kind of sites do I get?

A. You'll have a large number of websites to choose from with more and more added every week, including CPA review sites, multiple product review sites, digital product sites and squeeze pages. I've seen these templates myself and they are of excellent quality. It would take me days just to create one of them but these guys are churning them out FAST to help us out!

Q. Do the sites include legal details for FTC regulations?

A. Yes! Every site comes with all the pages you need, including a privacy policy and official statement that says that you're an affiliate promoting a product. This will keep you out of trouble from the FTC guys.

Q. Will I struggle with this?... I'm not that good with computers.

A. You don't need to be a technical genius to use this... you can actually be a technical dunce, because all you have to do is log in and follow the step-by-step wizard. It'll even put your site files on your web server for you, so you don't have to know anything about FTP.

Q. Can I use these sites to build my list?

A. Yes, absolutely. There are some very cool templates designed solely for list-building purposes and you'll be able to fully integrate your web-form capture code into them!

If you've got anymore questions, just contact the Instant Site Uploader team. They can answer any queries from you and membership spots are filling up fast!

Here's the official link:
http://www.emailmarketinginformer.com/recommends/instant-site-uploader

Imagine being able to create a nice-looking review site for some great affiliate products in a niche you want to target.

Imagine being able to do it without spending an arm and a leg on designers, graphic artists, copywriters and techie people to install everything for you.

Imagine being able to go from idea to complete website in 15-30 minutes.

That's what Instant Site Uploader lets you do. I think it's safe to say this is going to turn internet marketing upside down.

If you've been struggling to get past the hurdle that technical details put in the way of most people just getting started, this is EXACTLY what you need.

Here's the official link:
http://www.emailmarketinginformer.com/recommends/instant-site-uploader

Day 4 – FREE Forced Subscription Profits

SUBJECT: The '4 Letter Word' That Will Explode Your Potential - *FREE Download*

{!firstname_fix},

You've heard the expression "The money's in the list", but how exactly do you get a list in the first place?

How does one build a massive list, fast, quick and effortlessly without spending days, weeks, even months writing articles and doing tedious link-building?

Whilst you can set up a squeeze page and send traffic to it all day long using various methods there is another way.

=> The trick is to get others to do it for you!

It involves 'Forced Subscription' and a 4-letter word that will change the way you think about building a business!

You can simply throw a file or two out on the web and wait for it to come back to you with 100s more subscribers waiting to hear from you.. automatically!

I won't reveal too much, but you can get your copy of Aaron's report for absolutely nothing below;

Download your report here;
http://CLICKBANKID.fsprofits.hop.clickbank.net

Day 5 – No Money System

Hi {!firstname_fix},

When you think about starting a business, usually, some sort of investment comes into the equation right?

Maybe you think you at least need webhosting, or a domain name, or even an auto-responder right?

Whilst they will eventually form the building blocks of a strong business there is a more direct approach to making money online that allows you to get in, and get out without having to go through a checklist of things you could do with, but not at this very moment.

What if there was a way for even the *ABSOLUTE* novice to start from scratch with $0.00 in their pocket?..

Well with abundance of open source software, tagging websites, pinging services, video distribution sites and so on that is now a reality.

You've seen sites like YouTube, Squidoo, HubPages, MySpace, Digg, and more. They all have one thing in common. They're free! And very few marketers know how to use this to their advantage.

This *brand new* system makes use of all the latest web 2.0 gadgets, open source software and marketing techniques and turns it into a fully fledge marketing system.

...all of course, with *ZERO* investments!

You DO NOT need to have your own product...
You DO NOT need to have your own website...
You DO NOT need to have your own mailing list...
You DO NOT need to have any name recognition...
You DO NOT need to have any joint venture partners...
You DO NOT need to have a niche...
You DO NOT need to have extra money to spend on making this work...

Allow me to introduce to you the "No Money System"

http://CLICKBANKID.nomoneysys.hop.clickbank.net

Day 6 – Extra Max Cash

SUBJECT: How To Extract More From Your List?...

Hi {!firstname_fix},

I'm going to take a stab in the dark here and say that you've heard the following said somewhere on your internet travels...

"The money is in the list"

I'd like to challenge that. No the money is NOT in the list. It's in the QUALITY of the list.

Anyone can build (and buy for that matter) a large quantity of subscribers, but when it comes to promoting a product, they produce some appalling numbers.

No, the trick is not about how many subscribers you can get, it's what you DO with them that counts.

One marketer could have 10,000 on his list but get a 1% conversion when he sends out a promo email. Another marketer could have just 1000 on his list, but get a 20% conversion.

Who's going to bring in the most bacon?

Not only does it cost you more to store those leads, but your unsubscribe rates will be higher, and you'll be kicking yourself figuring out why someone with less subscribers manages to bring in more sales. Don't be the one with that 1% converting list!

List building is a system, however email

marketing is an art. What I'd like to share with you today is the art of extracting the maximum amount of cash from your existing mailing list and thinking less about filling up your auto-responder with dormant leads.

You can watch the first part of the video for free below:

http://CLICKBANKID.exmaxcash.hop.clickbank.net

Day 7 – Product Creator 1 Day 1

SUBJECT: *1* Thing All SUCCESSFUL Marketers Have In Common..

Hi {!firstname_fix},

Besides a list of subscribers, what is the one thing that all great marketers have in common?

..Their own product!

Yes! Every marketer has their own product and their own niche to promote their product to.

Not only that but they have their own affiliate program to allow others to promote their product too whilst earning a handsome commission!

Creating your own products needn't be hard, nor do you have to start from scratch as you're about to find out..

Here are my 6 tips to creating a successful product!

1. Target a hungry market.

You need to target desperate *BUYERS* and NOT freebie seekers! If you want your products to sell, get in front of people who are willing to spend by addressing their needs and problems!

2. Connect with your target market.

Before you develop your products, talk to your target market first. Visit the forums and ask them what answers they're looking for, what problems they're facing, even collect stories of their problems and use them as selling points on your sales letter.

3. Check on your competitors.

What kind of products do these people offer to their customers? What are their strengths and weaknesses? How do they market their products? What are they doing, what does their sales page look like? How can you outplay them?

4. Check on your resources.

You need to make sure that you have all what it takes to create your products. Are you going to do this alone? Are you starting from scratch, are you going to use PLR, can you afford to hire someone and how long do you have? Have a full plan first to avoid setbacks!

5. Charge appropriately.

Don't undercharge and don't be greedy. Ensure you're covering you time and out-goings whilst levelling up with your competitors. If you intend to charge more, you must be able to bring more value to your products such as gifts and bonuses.

6. Promote!

You're not going to make one sale if no one knows that your product exists! You need to implement multiple methods of generating traffic back to your website. You should be promoting with article submissions, social book-marking, directory submissions, press releases, video promos, blogging, pinging, setting up an affiliate program.. the lot!

This will ensure your product's success and

sustained flow of traffic for years to come.

So there you have it...6 rules for you to follow
when you come to create your own product....
*Target your niche
*Connect with your prospects
*Check out your competition
*Use what's already available
*Strategic pricing
*Promote promote promote!

Now you already know more than what 95% of other
marketers know!

If you want long term income and stable income
online, creating your own product is a must. The
trick is though; to be able to create multiple
high quality products that you can keep on
churning out to make more and more money online.

Whilst this product creation is a entire topic
onto itself, there is one home study course out
there that's packed with all the information you
need and has already had raving reviews from other
beginners.

It's called The 1 Day Product Creator is a full
blown home study course that will show you how to
create your own niche product from scratch in as
little as 1 day.

Once you've practiced this skill, you'll be able
to churn out site after site and build multiple
sources of income for yourself!

This is ONE skill that should not be overlooked!

Check it out here:
http://CLICKBANKID.1daypc.hop.clickbank.net

Day 8 – Product Creator 1 Day 2

SUBJECT: Everything You Need To Create A Successful Product Online

Hi {!firstname_fix},

If you have decided to create your first product online then I say to you congratulations!

You are now one step closer to earning a solid income online and taking back control from the Gurus that have been controlling the money game for too long.

The following are some of the areas that you will need to address as you put together your plan to create your first product.

The most important area you will need to look at is the market research area before you get started. I've covered some of this in previous emails but the name of the game here is making sure that there is a market for what you are selling. Don't make the mistake of creating a product and expending all your time and energy and something that no one wants. This is the crucial part.

Next you will need to create your product, whether it's a video series or eBook, you can get someone else to create it for you if you want.

The next step will be to create your website and your copy and to make sure that you have an affiliate page attached so you can attract a group of affiliates to sell your product you in the marketplace.

You are now ready to make money!

If the all of the above sounds like a lot of
work, you are right! There are many elements that
you will need to master if your product launch
online is to be a success.

If you would like to bypass this steep learning
curve and simply start creating winning products
in 24 hours from now, I have created a simple to
follow system that can show you how it's done.

If you haven't already done so, you can check out
this fantastic home study course that covers
EVERY aspect of product creation that will put
you ahead of the 95% who are still looking for
that magic bullet!

http://CLICKBANKID.1daypc.hop.clickbank.net

Day 9 – Sales Letter Factory 1

SUBJECT: How Your Sales Letter Can Make Or Break Your New Product

Today I want to talk about something which is often overlooked by a lot of marketers out there when they are creating their own product. As you may already know, having your own website is more than just the fancy header and footer, it's all about copy writing.

You may have done your niche research and made sure that there is a market for your product that is spending money in the area that you are going into.

You may be sitting there with a red hot idea and perhaps you have even created a list to sell it to, or you have people that you can sell it to through someone else's list.

If any of the above sounds familiar then congratulations! You are on the way to a successful product launch. But there is one thing to make sure you get right before you get ready to watch that money roll in-an area that is often overlooked in its importance .

I'm talking here about the sales letter. Get this part wrong and you will be leaving all your money and hard work on the table. The sales letter is your link to the customer and your chance to convince them that you have what they need. If this link in the chain is weak your customer will be lost. You must get the sales letter right in order to make a profit.

The trouble is though that getting the sales copy

right can take time and practise. You could of course outsource it to someone else but this can cost you upwards of $500 before you have made a single sale.

Fortunately though there is help at hand and you can produce high converting sales letters without having to hire a copywriter or roll the dice on all your hard work by writing your own copy.

With Sales Letters Factory you can produce some of the best sales letters in the business by simply pushing a few buttons and dragging and dropping some text.

Watch a video demonstration here to see how it works:

http://CLICKBANKID.slfactory.hop.clickbank.net

Day 10 – Sales Letter Factory 2

SUBJECT: 3 Things Your Sales Letter MUST Have To Make It Work

When a lot of people sit down to write the sales copy for their product they get confused as to what must go into it. You may wonder what ingredients and words will get those people clicking on the buy button and what will get them clicking off your page and looking at something else.

If you want to maximize the chances of someone buying your product {!firstname_fix} there are a number of key elements that you will need to incorporate in order to make it work for you. For the sake of simplicity I'm going to break these elements down into three parts. The first part is to tell them what you have, the second part is to tell them what it will do for them, and the third part is to get them to take action.

The first part starts with the headline where you have to outline the key benefit to the person. Make your headline specific and time centred to attract people more to your offer. For example "lose 10 lbs in a week using a 3 simple and safe techniques that will make your friends jealous" is more powerful than "lose weight".

Next you want to show how what you have can benefit them in their lives. You will need to marry their problem to your solution here. Social proof is a great way to show how you can really help them.

Finally you need tell them to take action and to buy from you. This is where a lot of people fail to complete the sale and lose money. You need to tell them what to do in order to buy from you.

If you follow the above structure you will at least have the basics to writing good copy. There is still however a lot of things that can go wrong.

If you want to make sure that you are putting together the right copy that will get you the sales that you need check out Sales Letters Factory where you can automate the whole process and come up with professional sales letters that will get you the results that you will need.

http://CLICKBANKID.slfactory.hop.clickbank.net

Day 11 – Cover Creator 1

SUBJECT: Why Creating Your Own Product Can Create Credibility

For a lot of people involved in the internet marketing business procrastination can be a real problem. There is just so much out there to choose from and you can get bombarded everyday with offers in your inbox where everything looks so attractive. You may have ideas swirling around your head about everything from eBay selling to membership sites to affiliate marketing.

There is however one thing that can really help you when if you are serious about making it in this business, and that is credibility. Nothing sells like credibility and reputation. When Frank Kern sells a product people are more interested in Frank Kern than the product itself. This is because of the reputation that he has built on the back of his product releases.

The bottom line is that nothing will build your credibility in this business like having your own product {!firstname_fix}. No matter how many other products you recommend to people that work out well for them, having a successful product that is linked to your name can build reputation like nothing else.

All you have to do is look around at the various gurus online and look at how their reputations have been built on the back of the products that they have created. You too can do the same.

When you are on your product creation journey you will encounter a number of things along the way that you will need to get right in order to preserve your reputation and improve your image online, and one of those things is the look of your website and eBook covers. There is no point having the best product that money can buy wrapped up in a shoddy unprofessional package.

If you want to find out how you can improve how people perceive you and your product online with slick, professional and easy to produce eCovers go now to 3D Cover Creator to check out how you can create your own professional eCovers in no time at all.

http://CLICKBANKID.3dcreator.hop.clickbank.net

Day 12 – Cover Creator 2

SUBJECT: Using 3D Virtual Covers To Make Sure Your Product Is A Success

Hi {!firstname_fix}, today I want to talk about some of the key things that you will need to do to make sure your product is a success.

The first thing you will need to do is to make sure that there is responsive market for the product that you selling.

Thankfully there a number of tools that you can use in this regard that are freely available online. To start with you could take a look at the likes of Amazon and look at the top one hundred products that are available for you online there. If your product idea is in line with one of the top one hundred product lines then things are looking good for you.

You could also access Google trends and keyword tools to make sure that there are people actively searching for what you want to sell. It's also a good idea to check out the likes of click bank and make sure that the product is falling into the main categories there. If you have a number of product creation ideas you could pick the category with the least amount of competition on click bank to maximise your chances of success.

Having the proper ground work like this in place is vital if you want to maximise your products chances for success online. There are other pieces to the puzzle too though.

After you do all the market research and go and create the product you will need to present it in the best possible way in order to maximise your chances of success. This is where a lot of marketers drop the ball and don't present their product in the best light. Don't make the same mistakes as them.

If you want to learn how you can create exceptional eCover images from your PC that will package your product in the best possible light, maximizing the sales possibility, head on over to 3D Cover Creator now to see how easily you can get it done.

http://CLICKBANKID.3dcreator.hop.clickbank.net

Day 13 – Easy Banner Creator 1

SUBJECT: How To Help Your Affiliates Sell Your Product!

Creating your own product and having it running live on your server is already a big achievement. But where many get thrown back is when they don't see the sales coming in. They expect something magical to happen and it should be selling itself.

I know you don't think like that {!firstname_fix}, or else you wouldn't be reading my emails would you? Just like any business, you need to recruit people to do the selling for you i.e. affiliates and providing them with the best material to help sell your product.

Having an army of affiliates in the trenches slogging away for you every day is one of the best ways to make money online. Like every army though they will need the best weapons at their disposal when they go out into the field. The better the weapons that you arm them with the more sales they will be able to bring for you.

One of the best things that you can give your affiliates is quality banners that they can easily put on their blogs and websites to get more click-throughs. Banners are one of the best ways to make sales conversions; opt in conversions and sign ups. Even Google has been using them more recently and are realising the power of the banner for getting more sales conversions and customers on board.

If you have tried to put banners together yourself you will know by now that the cost of a decent quality banner can be high and who wants to go learning all the ins and outs of Photoshop when you could be creating new products and attracting new affiliates to sell them.

The good news is though that if you can cut and paste and drag and drop, you are well on your way to making your own high quality banners that will stand out from the crowd and spread across websites making you money. With Easy Banner Creator you will be able can create your own high quality banners saving you a lot of time and effort.

Check it how easy it is to use this piece of software below:
http://CLICKBANKID.bancreator.hop.clickbank.net

Day 14 – Easy Banner Creator 2

SUBJECT: Create Cool Animated Banners With Simple Software!

If you were involved in internet marketing a few years ago you would know that the humble banner could rake in the cash for your everyday. In fact all you really needed to do to make sales was to pop up a banner on a site and wait for the sales to roll in. The better looking the banner, the better the sales that you got through it.

After a while though people developed what was known as "banner blindness" where the banners lost their effectiveness and marketers started to experiment with other ways of getting click-throughs to their offers.

The good news is though that banners have made a comeback and are increasing in popularity again. A well designed banner, put in the right area on your page can get as many if not more clicks as whatever text ad you are using.

If you would like some banners for your product but you don't fancy paying through the nose for a graphic designer then you'll want to check this out. Here's a simple solution for you to able to take advantage of the power of banners without all the hassle involved in getting them set up.

They can be created in literally minutes, all it takes is a few clicks, a drag and a drop and no previous graphic design experience is necessary.

http://CLICKBANKID.bancreator.hop.clickbank.net

Day 15 – Easy Banner Maker 1

SUBJECT: Easy Banner Creator Alternative! – *For Photoshop Users*

Hi {!firstname_fix},

A few days ago I sent out an email about a piece of software called Easy Banner Creator. A lot of my subscribers took me up on that offer, but I also have a few who wanted something that they could use with Photoshop.

If you didn't know already, Photoshop is the ultimate graphics tool that not only allows you to create brilliant looking websites, but also animated banners to.

Whilst Easy Banner Creator is a straight-forward piece of software that gets the job done, some want the absolute best with PSD templates already made for them.

Which is exactly what this email is all about.

If you're a big fan of Photoshop you can now grab a collection of un-flattened PSD templates that allow you to modify separate layers, animate and stylize to your custom needs.

You'll be able to add your own text, images, move things around and much more. Everything is already nicely laid out for you, and you can customize EVERYTHING you see on the banners.

They come in the standard banner formats 120x600, 250x250, 200x200, 468x60, 120x240, 180x150, 125x125, 234x60 and there's even some extra graphics elements included to polish up your websites.

Watch the video demonstration below:
http://CLICKBANKID.banmaker.hop.clickbank.net

Day 16 – Copy Paste Audio 1

SUBJECT: Audio Is Powerful – Here's How To Use It!

Today I want to talk about another element of product creation that can make a serious impact on your sales figures. I'm talking here about the use of sound.

When you are trying to sell to your prospect online the key thing that you will need to do is to engage with them and most people will do this with the use of a website and the copy that is on the site.

This can work fine but if you are going down this road you are leaving out a big opportunity to connect more with your buyer and create more sales. With the use of audio on your website you can change all this and connect more with your buyer. There are a number of reasons for this.

Sounds that we hear are very powerful and can enter into the subjects mind and control what they do. If you doubt this just look at Paul Mc Kenna or any famous hypnotist and watch how they can control people by simply talking to them. When you talk to your customers you influence their buying decision more as you will be talking to their sub conscious mind.

People are fundamentally always looking for the easy, less painful option in life and if they can sit back and watch a sales page that has audio they will do this instead of reading through a long sales letter. The combination of audio and text works best as this will give them something to listen to and to read before they make a buying decision.

The trouble though with learning something new is that it can take time and effort and your schedule is probably pretty full up if you are involved in internet marketing. If you hire out the job to someone else it can also cost you big time, which you don't want to do before you have sold any product.

Luckily though there is a solution where you can get the best of both worlds and get top class audio and integrated into your site without programming skills and without spending a fortune by following some simple cut and paste steps. http://CLICKBANKID.cpaudio.hop.clickbank.net

Day 17 – Build Affiliate Army 1

SUBJECT: How To Get Other People To Make Money For You

When you create a product online for sale you basically have 2 courses of action that you can follow.

You can first of all look at doing all the promotion yourself and keep all the commissions for yourself or you could get together an army of affiliates to do the work for you.

If you want to get out of the trenches and command an army of affiliates you will make more money long term as you will have people promoting your site for you and when you leverage the power of other people like this and scale things up it can be very lucrative for you {!firstname_fix}.

The trouble is all your efforts may have gone into creating your product and now you have to go and find the affiliates. The following are some tips that will help you find these people and get them promoting for you.

The first thing to do is to make sure your product is listed in a market place like click bank or pay dot come where affiliates can get access to your product in order to promote it. You will then need to make sure that you have an affiliate page where you will have affiliate tools for them to use.

Affiliates are far more likely to promote your product if you give them the tools straight up in order to do so. These tools will include things like graphics where they can put their affiliate links and reviews that they can post on their blogs. You could also look at giving them keywords they can use in their articles or ad words campaigns.

If you want to gather a team of affiliates to help you with your product you will also need to go hunting for them and there are a variety of methods you can use to help you with this. If your product is in the IM sector there are a number of sites out there where you can find JV partners for your launch and if it's in another sector you can also find affiliates on a variety of different forums and sites out there that will promote for you.

The Trouble with creating products online though is that time can be against you, especially if you are doing everything yourself. Having the right affiliates on board though can literally mean the difference between success and failure online. While they are busy selling your product you will be able to go about creating new products and can be expanding your business.

Watch the first video below to pick up some free tips on how to build your own affiliate of affiliates:

http://CLICKBANKID.buildarmy.hop.clickbank.net

Day 18 – PDF Brandable

Subject: *NEW* PDF Branding Tool Just Released!

Hi {!firstname_fix},

If you've bought any of my products before you'll know that I place a lot of emphasis on my affiliate programs.

Sometimes I do get lazy and place a 'coming soon' on the affiliate page but either way when I do create one, I provide my affiliates with as many tools possible to make sure they start promoting that very same day.

And out of all the tools I provide, the most important one is giving them the ability to rebrand a PDF.

Why?...

Rebranding PDFs is quick and easy to do
They're easy to share and get passed around
They cost little or nothing to create
They can pre-sell the reader
They're a great way to get free traffic
You affiliates don't have to edit everything manually and recompile the report
They're a viral promoters, especially if it's valuable, controversial or entertaining!

and finally...

They bring you SALES!

In a rush?...
http://CLICKBANKID.pdfbrand.hop.clickbank.net

You see, unlike an article, or an email, or an animated banner, eBooks and reports allow you to show who you really as a business and what you can provide.

Your report could be a tutorial on how to use of software... a review of a product you bought... a mind-map or blueprint to a problem... or even just a short snippet of the original product.

Either way, they are designed for the reader to check out where that report came from so they can visit your website without being pushed into a sale. It's a great way to pre-sell potential customers whilst making your affiliates look good and making their lives easier.

Put simply making your PDFs BRANDABLE works. I use them everywhere I can and let my affiliates do the selling for me.

Now you can try this affiliate resource technique yourself...

http://CLICKBANKID.pdfbrand.hop.clickbank.net

Day 19 – FREE Setup My Resell Rights 1

SUBJECT: *FREE* 2Hr Webinar Reveals Secrets To Resell Rights - Must Watch!

Hi {!firstname_fix},

If you haven't heard of the term 'resell rights'
on your internet travels it's either because
a) you're completely new online or b) the thought
of setting up a website and selling it online
scares you!

It's nothing to be ashamed of - I know this because
I couldn't even understand what 'resell rights' meant
let alone how to use them!

That was until I watched Chris and Aaron's
'Setup My Resell Rights' site.

In a rush?...
http://CLICKBANKID.setupmyrr.hop.clickbank.net

Just as the website name suggests, this site is
dedicated entirely to setting up your resell rights
products rather than having lying around on your
hard drive collecting dust!

You'll learn how to...

- set up a PayPal buy now button
- set up auto-redirect after transactions
- turn on auto-delivery in PayPal
- edit your sales page (index.html)
- edit your download/thank you page
- set your pricing
- upload to your server with FTP
- understand the mini-site file structure

and so much more..

I was really impressed with the content
which is why I had to email you today.

Here's the link:
http://CLICKBANKID.setupmyrr.hop.clickbank.net

P.S. You'll have to hurry because I don't
know how much longer this videos will be
available!

P.P.S. I can assure you, once you've gone
through this one videos, you'll never have
to ask anyone about setting up and modifying
a resell rights product ever again!

Day 20 – FREE Setup My Resell Rights 2

SUBJECT: Last Chance To Enter The Webinar {!firstname_fix}!

Hi {!firstname_fix},

If you read my previous Email you'll be aware of how having the ability to create and modify resell rights products can make a world of difference to your online success!

'Resell rights' is nothing new, in fact, they've been around for a very long time, but finding a good quality products (ones that you stand a chance of making sales on) are very hard to find.

You'll either have to search the net for ages, pay a hefty premium, or create them from scratch. And then there's the issue of setting them up to collect sales.

Take a breather...

You won't need to do either because Aaron is providing a full 2hr video on setting up your products as well as providing a ready-to-go product - absolutely free!

Download here:
http://CLICKBANKID.setupmyrr.hop.clickbank.net

P.S. This will be the last time you'll hear from me regarding this course, but I really feel it's important for you to know because it's helped me take control of my business and given me direction which is why I'm telling you today!

Email Marketing Informer

Day 21 – FREE Resale Rights Ninja

SUBJECT: *FREE* MRR Business In A Box! – Instant Download

Have you ever wondered how some marketers seem to
be able to produce product after product and turn
a profit almost without breaking a sweat?...

Or how you can quickly take advantage of that
profitable niche you've just found?...

Creating a product from scratch takes time. If
you add in research and setting up the backend,
it can take anything from a week or two or even
more. If you outsource product development, it is
unlikely to be much faster.

It is also a LOT of work creating a product, and
to be honest with you {!firstname_fix}, many
marketers have no idea where to start. Creating a
product can be a complex process that takes time
and effort.

But what if there was a way for you to create a
product almost instantly with very little work
and in some cases, with no work?

What if there was a way for you to profit from
other people's effort for pennies on the dollar
compared to what it would cost you to hire them
directly?

What I'm about to give you will change your
perspective on resell rights products and will
open up your mind to new possibilities.

Now because you're on my list, I've convinced
Aaron to do me this ONE favour. This is a REAL
video training product that currently costs $27

but you'll be able to get it for absolutely
nothing.

Follow the link below and you'll be redirected
straight to the download page. No sign-ups, no
special offers or anything else involved. Just
great content from a very generous guy.

Grab it below whilst it's still available:
http://www.resellrightsninja.com/RRNinja_DL.html

P.S. Better still, he's providing you with Master
Resell Rights to this product so you'll have an
instant business-in-a-box! How cool is that?!

Day 22 – Web 2.0 Resell Rights

SUBJECT: 5x Video Resell Rights Products In A Box Now Available!

{!firstname_fix},

When it comes to making money (online and offline) there are two factors that are vitally important. Time and effort.

Your time is valuable and you want to spend your time doing what you're good at. If you're good at closing JV deals, you do that, if you're good at creating sale page videos, you do that, if you're good at emailing your list you do that.

The big mistake is attempting to do everything yourself. The last thing you want do for example do is spend your precious time attempting to design a mini-site header and get a B+ at best when you could hire someone else to get it done is half the time and give you A+ results.

The same applies with effort. Why attempt to do something from scratch when someone has already done the work for you. Don't try to reinvent the wheel when it's easier to work with it.

Smart use of your time combined with clever use of what's already available is what will set you apart from other marketers.

This is what today's email is all about.

Aaron has just released a quality set of Resell Rights video products which you can sell to the end user.

In a rush?...
http://CLICKBANKID.web20rr.hop.clickbank.net

You'll get access to 5 mini-site businesses-in-a-box. Each come with their own fully written sales page, ready-linking download page, awesome graphics and a quality video series teach beginners the basics of internet marketing such as:

• How to set up their own membership • List building • Article marketing • Social networking • and creating affiliate programs

If you've ever bought any of Aaron's resell rights products before you'll know that he spends a lot of time making them look good and always sell like hotcakes.

His new pack is no exception. You'll be able to download your business-in-a-box, add your name to it, slap on your own PayPal button and then promote to your own subscribers. It's a great way to bring in extra income and an even better way to place you as the expert without having to read/write or research any of the material yourself… truly lazy if you ask me.. but hey, that's the name of the game. More money, less effort.

So if you haven't already done so, check out the 5 businesses-in-a-box and watch the sample videos to really see what you're getting:

http://CLICKBANKID.web20rr.hop.clickbank.net

Day 23 – PLR Profit Made Easy

SUBJECT: Old PLR From 2005 Still Sells Today! - FREE Video Shows How!

Hi {!firstname_fix},

No matter how many times you've been told that you need to "create your own products" to be successful online, there will be some people who will just not grasp the concept.

They either think it's...

a) too hard
b) too time consuming
c) too expensive
d) not worth it
e) or some other excuse..

The truth is, you can still create your own products but without having to put in all the unnecessary hard work and time-consuming effort to produce the results I'm about to show you.

His name is John Thornhill and he has been online since 1999, which is a long time in terms of internet marketing so he knows a thing or two when it comes launching new products from PLR content.

One of his sites (revealed in the video) generated $1971.97 in 7 days since its launch, with a peak of $728.83 in a single day and has also built a list of 246 buying customers.

And that was just in the first 7 days... those numbers will continue to grow!

In this 12 minute video he'll reveal to you...

- A live example of how an old out-of-date
product was revamped in something completely new!

- Logging in live into one of his ClickBank accounts
to see the stats just for this product!

- The daily figures of when he launched the PLR
product, where it peaked, and how it will
continue to grow!

- How and why he managed to get 100s of links
pointing back to my site after the initial launch.

- Why other PLR sellers continuously fail because
they forget one important rule.

And did I forget to mention, all this information
is FREE in this need-to-see 12 minute video!

Watch the video below...
http://CLICKBANKID.plrpme.hop.clickbank.net

Day 24 – Pay a Professional 1

SUBJECT: How To Leverage Off Other People's Time So You Can Grow

Hi {!firstname_fix},

By now you'll be aware of how much work is involved when it comes to making money online. There's product creation, creating promotional material for your affiliates, ensuring your site is in working order, list-building, getting traffic, link building and so much more.

And with all these important to-do tasks it can be hard at times to focus on getting just ONE simple task done. If you are feeling tired or even a little bit burnt out let me assure you that you're not alone! There are many marketers out there at the moment that are feeling the same way including myself!

Here's the thing though, there are basically two ways to do business online. You can try to do everything yourself or you can outsource your activities and leverage the power of other people in your endeavours.

If you decide to go with the second option here you will be making more money in the long term and the reason for this is simple. You are in effect limited to what you can achieve online as an individual but your ability to employ other people and the results that they can achieve for you is unlimited and that means that the limits to which you can grow your business are unlimited.

When it comes to outsourcing your business though, a lot of people find it difficult to find the right people at the right price that you can partner with to grow your business. Again you have two choices here in that you can go it alone and see how you get on with the freelancer sites out there or you can take the lead from someone who has outsourced most of their work and knows about the many pitfalls that are involved in this business.

If you have made the decision to outsource your business you will be aware that time is the most valuable commodity that you have online so why waste more time trying to figure out all the pitfalls of outsourcing yourself.

If you want to learn how to start delegating work to other people, free up your time, allow you to focus on more important task – such as building more websites and growing your business then this new video series on outsourcing is going to help.

http://CLICKBANKID.payapro.hop.clickbank.net

Day 25 – Profit Lens 1

SUBJECT: "I Need Traffic – What Do I Do?"

If you have put in the time and effort into creating your product you will need to make sure that you maximize your efforts online by making sure that you are getting traffic to your offer.

Getting traffic is one of the things that beginner's leave to last because they a) find it easy to work on their website and get from basic HTML done or b) have already tried to do a few things but saw little or no effects and gave up.

What you need to understand is that there are many traffic generation strategies out there at the moment that can help you get those valuable customers to your site but few are more powerful then constructing articles on Web 2.0 social networks like Squidoo!

The great thing about Web 2.0 properties like Squidoo, Hub Pages etc is that they already have a high pr ranking with Google so it's easy for you to get on the front page of Google for whatever keywords you are trying to rank for.

Getting your Squidoo lens seen online starts with doing the right keyword research and finding a main keyword and associated or lsi keywords to rank for. I usually check on Google and see if there is a squidoo lens ranking there already on the front page as I believe Google likes variety and is more likely to rank your lens on the front page is there is not one there already.

I would also put the keyword you want to rank for in quotes and scroll right to the end to get the true number of competition pages for those keywords. You can place your main and LSI keywords in the keyword section while you are constructing your lens to maximise the chance of it being seen online. To give your lens extra juice with Google you should use pingoat to ping it when finished and you should also social bookmark the lens.

These steps above will give you a good grounding in how to get started with your Squidoo lenses but if you want to save yourself time and money and you want to avoid the mistakes that most marketers make then there's a full video course entirely dedicated to this subject to help you.

http://CLICKBANKID.squidoogen.hop.clickbank.net

Day 26 – GTP System 1

SUBJECT: A Brand New Traffic Method You Need To Know About.

Let me ask you a question {!firstname_fix}, are
you sick of all the old traffic generation
strategies being bandied about by all the gurus
out there while you are still trying to get
traffic to your site.

Things like article marketing, Face Book,
Twitter, YouTube, blogging, back-linking, and
social bookmarking. If so then you are not alone.

Sometimes my head spins from all the methods out
there and what's worse is that all I want to get
is a result for my efforts fast. Don't get me
wrong, the other forms of traffic generation
still work but I'm impatience by nature and I
want things done as fast as possible. As they say
time is money and when you're waiting for traffic
to come to your website so you can start making
sales then the saying doesn't hold much truer.

I have recently discovered a way to get traffic
that most internet marketers know nothing about.
This is essentially a way to get unlimited
traffic to your site and an unlimited amount of
inbound links to boost your rankings in Google.

This method is nothing to do with any of the
traffic methods mentioned above or any traffic
generation strategy you have heard of. It is
however the most powerful method I have
discovered for getting traffic to my sites and to
make more cash than I have in years.

Watch the video below to a brief blueprint of the
system:

http://CLICKBANKID.gtpsys.hop.clickbank.net

Day 27 – PPC 4 Treasure 1

SUBJECT: How To INJECT More Traffic With PPC

Hi {!firstname_fix},

If you're desperate to get traffic fast and are not afraid to spend a little doing so because you know that you've got an excellent product that people really want, then you may want to consider PPC.

PPC stands for Pay Per Click and is exactly as it implies. You write a small text ad, choose the keywords you want your ad to be display for, and then have it displayed on the search results of sites like Google, Yahoo, MSN and Bing.

These PPC networks allow you to track your campaign performance as well so when you generate a conversion – either a sale or a sign-up you'll know exactly how much it cost you to acquire that action.

How is that useful?... Well if you have a product selling for $100 and it cost you $50 in clicks to generate that sale, you know that for every $50 you spend, you'll receive $100 back. Nice deal isn't it :)

When done correctly you'll be able to scale up your business faster, and send in more traffic from more paid sources and this is just one of many way some marketers make a living online.

However PPC is tricky and if you don't keep an eye on your campaigns you can wind up losing a lot of money and there are a number of elements that you must get right if this traffic method is to work for you.

One of the key things you will need to pay attention to is where your ad gets placed or where it gets ranked. Even if you have the best crafted ad in the world all your efforts can go to waste if it doesn't get ranked well.

The ranking of your ad will ultimately depend on how much you are paying per click and your quality score. Ultimately your quality score will depend upon things like the historical click through rate of the ad, the click through rate of the display URLs and the performance geographically of ads in the area, among other things.

Ultimately your control over the situation will depend upon you making sure that your ad has as much relevance as possible in it's key wording, geographical location and anywhere else you can demonstrate this to Google.

PPC can be a wonderful traffic method but like every other method of driving traffic there can be a steep learning curve involved. If you would like to skip the pain involved with failed campaigns, Google slaps and wasted money, I have discovered a way to get thousands of visitors to your site through PPC that won't break the bank. This method is simple, fast and effective and you can be up and running in minutes from now.

What I've got for you is a 14-part video series entirely on the subject which will make you more proficient in getting traffic. You can watch the first video below:

http://CLICKBANKID.ppc4treas.hop.clickbank.net

Day 28 – Click Drag Graphics 1

SUBJECT: Click Drag And Drop For Amazing Website Graphics!

{!firstname_fix}, let me ask you something…

Have you ever outsourced your graphics? How much money have you spent on hiring graphic designers? How long have you been waiting for your final design after sending emails back and forth for revisions?

Good graphics come at a premium and revisions cost even more especially to get it to look the way you want it.

Designers my charge $97 just for 1 eBook cover, expect even more if you want a group package of your product.

It can become quite costly and even though you know you need to outsource the graphics, it sometimes is a good idea to do them yourself, let the sales come in, then upgrade the graphics at a later date.

We all know how important graphics are to any website. Graphics are what makes a website come alive. They grab the reader's attention. They sell products and services. No matter what it is that you are trying to sell online, you must have professional looking graphics.

Without professional looking graphics, you simply cannot compete online.

That's all well and good, you may be saying to yourself; but I'm not a graphic designer. I have absolutely zero experience in graphic design.

That's the situation where most people find themselves and that is precisely why they throw away a fortune on hiring professional graphic designers. Because they think they do not have any choice. That's the myth that graphics designers continue to perpetuate because they don't want people like us to discover the real truth. The real secret.

Here's the real secret: you don't need any experience to create stunning graphic designs.

All you need to be able to do is click and drag.

Yep. That's right. And graphics designers know it too. They're just hoping you don't figure it out so you will continue to pay them thousands of dollars to do exactly the same thing you could do on your own if you only knew it was available.

That's what I want to share with you. Click Drag Graphics gives you everything you need to be able to create stunning graphics in just minutes without any experience at all. I'm not kidding. All you have to be able to do is click and drag. If you can do that, you can create your own graphics in no time.

You can even customize and resize your graphics. How much would a graphic designer charge you to go back and make changes?

You do the math.

Watch a quick video demo here:
http://CLICKBANKID.cdgraphics.hop.clickbank.net

Day 29 – Push Button Lazy Marketer

SUBJECT: Automate Tedious Tasks With This 1 Software…

{!firstname_fix},

We all know how much potential is available in Internet marketing. It's a wide open field. But, if you're like most people, you probably find yourself spending more time than you would like handling all of those boring, routine tasks. Handling email, checking stats, writing content, getting your websites built. All of those things that are so essential to successful marketing, but really bog you down and make it difficult to move on to other things. Or enjoy the fruits of your labor.

No one signs up to spend that much time on their computer. After all, that's supposed to be one of the benefits of running your own business, harnessing the power of the Internet, right? Being able to get more out of life, enjoy more free time? The problem is; all of those mundane tasks seem to take over until you're spending more time managing those than enjoying life.

The key is being able to put your business on automated pilot so that all of those routine tasks are handled for you.

Wait a minute, you might be thinking to yourself. That sounds great, but you can't really do that. Can you?

The answer is, actually, yes you can. Computers were designed to make life easier, right? So, why is that we spend so much time acting as virtual slaves to them? There has to be a better way and now it has been discovered.

How would you like to be able to press a single button and have your computer automatically handle a task that would normally take you eight hours to complete?

Seriously.

That is precisely what a new revolutionary software program is able to do. Completely customize all of those repetitive, boring tasks that you are currently dedicating so much of your timer to completing. Instead of playing with your kids, hanging out with your friends, spending quality time with your significant other; you know, all of the things that make life worthwhile.

"Push-Button Lazy Marketer" puts you in control of your time and how you spend it. If you value your time and if you want to get more done in less time, this is the one tool that you absolutely cannot do without. Imagine being able to create product reviews, handle emails, design website templates, automatically perform quick searches and all of those other tasks that take up so much time, in just a few minutes instead of spending hours on them. That's the freedom you get with the Push Button Lazy Marketer.

http://CLICKBANKID.pblazy.hop.clickbank.net

Day 30 – Video Brander Elite

SUBJECT: $45,852 Just By Branding Videos... A Must See!

{!firstname_fix},

We all know that video is one of the hottest and most powerful selling tools online today. You don't need me to tell you that. Without video, you're leaving money on the table. Up until recently, the full potential of videos was not really exploited. They're great for testimonials or if you want to make your own little web infomercial.

If you use affiliate marketing, video really would not benefit you much because there simply was not a way to refer a sale from them. You could use them for testimonials, but that really wouldn't help you much as an affiliate marketer. When used in the right way, a video page can be a powerful selling tool. In fact, it can practically do all the work for you by pre-selling the product you're marketing.

The Internet is rapidly evolving. If you want to stay ahead of the competition you have to stay ahead of the curve and act on the latest tools and techniques. That's why you simply cannot afford to ignore the power of video, even if you're an affiliate marketer. Especially if you are an affiliate marketer.

So, what options are left open to you if you want to tap into that power but you do not have any experience in creating videos? The secret lies in video branding. What is that? If you're not familiar with video branding, the basic idea behind it is taking an existing video and

branding it with your own info to make it
uniquely yours. Here's how it works:

Choose a video. Enter an affiliate link. Upload,
brand and you're done!

It's really that simple. You do not need your own
video and you certainly do not need any
experience in creating videos. If you can type,
you can brand your own videos and start using
them to take your profits to the next level.

Why let everyone else walk away with all of the
profits while you sit idly by and think to
yourself "If only I could use videos…." Now you
can. Use your own videos. Use existing videos.
The secret to getting massive amounts of traffic
today is video.

Video Brander Elite gives you the power to make
use of the hottest tool on the Internet today.
Find out how you can give your profits a kick
start with video today!

http://CLICKBANKID.vbelite.hop.clickbank.net

Day 31 – My Social Business

SUBJECT: Your Own Social Network Site! – Script Now Available!

{!firstname_fix},

I want you to imagine just for a second what it would be like to own a "NICHE" social networking site that had thousands of active visitors.

You've got people signing up for a new account every day. You've got existing members posting real fresh content on your site. And then you've got Google giving you high rankings for keywords that you didn't even mean to target and then you've got the full control to display AdSense ads, ClickBank ads and much more where ever you want.

Seriously how cool would that be?...

It's list-building, niche marketing, content-building, and monetization all in one.

Also notice that I said "niche" social networking site. I want you to really process that because it's highly important. This is not the same old internet marketing stuff – we're talking about creating a site that people feel passionately about and spend hours on end discussing and socializing to each other about... all whilst you sit back and let the content within your site grow!

How much traffic do you think you could make from your chosen niche or niches if you could setup a social MySpace style site specifically for that niche?

I think we both know the answer to that is "a ton of high quality traffic".

Now for the first time, there is a script that allows you to build a site just like that. You design it, you say who it's built for and you let it work for you.

Forget tedious link building, article marketing, and mini-site creation for a second – this is what the core of the web is all about, interaction!

And you'll be able to pull this all off with one piece of software! Check it out:

http://CLICKBANKID.snbuilder.hop.clickbank.net

Day 32 – CPA 4 Newbies

SUBJECT: $4, $10, $50, Even $200 Just For Gettin Traffic To Sign-Up!

Hi {!firstname_fix},

You're already fully aware that you can make money by selling your own products. You're already fully aware that you can sell other people's products as an affiliate. And you also know that you can display ads on your website such as AdSense to generate revenue.

It's a well known fact that the Internet is a gold mine just waiting to be taken advantage of. If you have a product or service. At least, that's what most people think.

What most people don't realize is that it's a big myth that you need something to sell to tap into the incredible potential of the Internet.

There is now a new and more frictionless way of bringing in an income online. You only have to send traffic to an opt-in page and if they sign up, you get commissioned.

The secret is CPA. Cost Per Action Marketing.

Haven't heard of it?

Right now, CPA is the easiest and fastest way for even a complete newbie to break into Internet marketing and begin raking in cash.

What's so different about CPA?

First off, I want to tell you that CPA is

different from anything else you may have tried or considered. With affiliate marketing, you usually put an offer up on your website. A visitor then clicks on your ad and makes a purchase. You get a portion of the sale as your commission. In other words, you do not make any money unless someone buys something.

CPA marketing is completely different. You do not have to sell anything with CPA. That's right. You read it right. No one has to buy anything for you to make money with CPA.

All that have to do is take a specific action. When they do, you earn a commission. You can make money when they do something as simple and as easy as filling in their email address or zip code.

This is what is so great about CPA. You don't have to spend your time or energy trying to convince someone to spend their hard earned money. All you have to do is convince them to take one simple action. Do that and you make money.

Now, I do want to tell you that while CPA Marketing is absolutely a fast and easy way to make money, you can't just rush into it. You have to be prepared. The reason is that CPA networks are pretty adept at spotting a newbie. Some networks won't even accept your application if you do not have a proven record.

CPA 4 Newbies is a must have if you want to succeed with CPA. It tells you everything you need to know about the entire application process and even how you can help you get accepted.

Watch an introduction video below:

http://CLICKBANKID.cpa4newb.hop.clickbank.net

Day 33 – Dynamite Trends

SUBJECT: A Cool Technique You Can Use In Emergencies

Hi {!firstname_fix},

We all know how important it is to choose a niche. Choose the right niche and you can be on your way toward a life of financial independence. Choose the wrong niche and you're back to answering to someone else.

The key to choosing the right niche lies in being able to keep your finger on the pulse of emerging trends and respond at the right time. Tapping into those niches that have yet to be uncovered. Knowing what is going on right now, on a daily basis and sometimes even an hourly basis can literally make the difference between untold riches and answering to someone else for the rest of your life.

Internet marketing has become more and more lucrative. It's also become extremely competitive. That means that in order to stay in the game you absolutely must be able to uncover those trends and take action at the right time. What's the good in knowing that something was a trend after the fact when everyone else has already jumped on it?

To succeed you need to be able to predict the trends so you can be the first one out of the gate.

The problem that many Internet marketers face, especially when they are first starting out, is that they cannot afford to spend any extra money or time on researching niches and trends. Suppose for a moment that you could do the following:

1.   Identify a fantastic trend
2.   Research that trend
3.   Set up a FREE blog on that trend with content
4.   Monetize the blog for highly targeted traffic
5.   Drive the targeted traffic to that trend blog
6.   Maintain records for all of those

Rinse. Repeat. In other words, do it over and over again; all the while making a profit as each new trend emerges.

What if you could spend about an hour per project and start watching the profits rolling in? Does that sound like something you could do?

Most people never realize that everything they need to do precisely what I just described is available online and for FREE!

As a result, they waste precious time, money and resources and still never achieve their full potential.

Dynamite Trends shows you how to harness those resources that are available online absolutely for FREE and reveals how to put them to work for you in a simple six step program that can be easily replicated again and again for incredible profits.

Watch the first part of the system below:
http://CLICKBANKID.dmtrends.hop.clickbank.net

Day 34 – Secret Sales Affiliate

SUBJECT: Affiliate Marketing With Amazon… Does It Work?

It seems like everyone has a get rich quick scheme today they want to sell you. That's because the Internet is without a doubt one of the richest opportunities that exists today.

When you have the right tools at your side, you can establish a successful and profitable home business. The problem is that there are so many products and opportunities available out there it can be hard to sort through all of the scams and find the real gems. It's become so bad that many people have just given up on the idea of trying to make money online.

The truth is that there ARE a lot of scams out there. Usually, there's only one person really making money from a lot of those programs and it's the person trying to sell it to you! Despite all of that, there are some honest, proven methods for making money online. People have been able to make enough money online that they were able to quit their day jobs and begin living the good life. How have they done it?

Affiliate marketing.

Okay, so if affiliate marketing is so great, why isn't everyone jumping on the band wagon?

You can make money with affiliate marketing, but you have to be able to figure out where to start. You have to know which affiliates are the best to begin with, how to choose a product and then how to identify the appropriate keywords to start generating traffic once you have your website established. I'm not going to kid you. It's not as easy as everyone makes it sound. There are several steps involved and you have to know how to use the right strategies. That is why everyone hasn't quit their day jobs and retired to a private island somewhere. They just simply do not know where to get started and where to go once they do get started.

Secret Sales Affiliate shows you everything you need to know to get started with affiliate marketing. With this step by step program, you can literally start generating income within just a few days. Whether you're looking to make a little extra money or you have an eye towards building your own business, this series of videos will show you precisely what to do. All you need is the time and willingness to learn and then put the strategies into place.

http://CLICKBANKID.ssaffiliate.hop.clickbank.net

Day 35 – Make Decisions Now

SUBJECT: Why Most People Fail Online?...

{!firstname_fix}, let me ask you something, and answer honestly here...

How many times have you sat in front of the TV and said to yourself 'I should really be working on my online business'... when really you only continued sitting in front of the TV, flicking through channels, looking for something that you 'must watch' and making up excuses to yourself that you just didn't have enough time?

How many times have you said that you've got to do something, made a mental note of it and possibly even planned your day ahead only to be distracted from friends, family or colleagues?

How many times have you actually got down to work, but found it so hard to concentrate and get any real tasks done that you eventually gave up and started chatting on the forums?

Seriously how many times has that happened to you?... It's all happened to us at some point in our lives - so don't worry, we're all in the same boat.

It's no secret that you have to work to achieve your goals. Without working toward the achievement of your goals, you simply will never get there.

Don't get me wrong, I'm not saying that the only option is grueling, back breaking work to get from where you are to where you want to be.

Thankfully, that's not the case either!

What you need to do is combine hard work along with techniques for effective decision making to make progress toward your goals. The combination of these creates a synergetic approach which helps you achieve your goals faster and much easier.

It goes without saying that decision making is one of, if not the most, important factors in determining success in life, business, relationships, and emotions.

Sadly, the majority of people in the world suffer with wishy-washy decision making that doesn't move them toward their goals but keeps them floundering instead! Most people sit on important decisions for hours, days, weeks, and even months or years when a fast decision would have been more than ample. The stress comes from over analyzation of a decision and wanting to make the "perfect" decision. This usually results in no decision which means NO results!

So what I want to do today is help you when it comes to making decisions and taking action by sharing with you some tricks I use.

You can watch the intro video below:
http://CLICKBANKID.makedecnow.hop.clickbank.net

Looking for a Special Bonus to really compliment this book?

Step 1: Visit www.JonCrimes.com

Step 2: Sign up to receive the free Email Series

Step 3: Get a PDF copy of this book and….

Step 4: Your great Free Bonus!

P.S. You're going to love it!

www.ingramcontent.com/pod-product-compliance
Lightning Source LLC
Chambersburg PA
CBHW051507170526
45166CB00001B/426